Papercraft

Papercraft

Pamela Woods

Line artwork by Marilyn Day

Hamlyn
London · New York · Sydney · Toronto

Acknowledgements

The author would like to acknowledge the generous help of
Valerie Jackson, Vanessa Woods, Julia Morland, Nora Pearse
and Caroline Morrison in enthusiastically producing some of
her designs.
She would also like to thank Arthur Sanderson & Sons Ltd.
(papers), Hunky Dory Designs (papers), Gallery Five Ltd.
(papers), Paperchase Ltd. (papers), Gainsborough Press
(Noah's Ark), But is it Art (boxes), Daler Board (mounting
board), Peter Bates Limited (picture frames), George
Rowney & Co. Ltd. (paints), and Porth Textiles Limited
(Christmas materials) for their encouragement and expert
help.

The editor would like to thank Cassell Ltd. for permission to
use the quote on page 42.
Endpapers in New England design by Juliet Glynn Smith
© 1976 Hunkydory Designs Limited.
Wallpaper in the photograph on page 26 by Laura Ashley.

Photographs on pages 118 and 122 by Michael Plomer
Remaining photographs by Paul Williams

First published in 1979 by
The Hamlyn Publishing Group Limited
London · New York · Sydney · Toronto
Astronaut House, Feltham, Middlesex, England

Filmset in England by Photocomp Ltd., Birmingham
in 10 on 11pt. Rockwell Light

Printed in Italy
ISBN 0 600 37192 1

Contents

Introduction

Paper is an intriguing material and surprisingly delicate considering the huge trees and other matter from which it comes. The craft of paper-making originated in China in the first century A.D., was enthusiastically taken up by the Japanese and later spread westwards. The process of paper-making is highly mechanised today but there are still some lacy Japanese hand-made papers available and at Whookey Hole in Somerset it is possible to see hand-made paper being produced in a paper mill which has been restored to its original state.

The Victorians were keen paper workers and applied their creative minds to producing elaborate and detailed decorations and some of their artefacts remain as an example to inspire us. Papercraft is by no means a new subject but given fresh thought, based on past masters, this book sets out to explore the possibilities that paper offers.

In its finished form paper is a crisp, firm material, though sometimes flimsy. It requires direct and positive manipulation for three dimensional work but must always be handled carefully. Where paper is to be joined, glue is normally the means employed.

As it is made of compressed pulp it reverts to this state when wet, forming papier-mâché which can also be used for craft work.

The book begins by giving general information on the types of paper available and general methods of working it. This is followed by a selection of designs and plans for the craftsman. These include some simple items for the beginner in earlier chapters and more elaborate designs in later chapters which draw on the experience previously gained.

Over fifty designs in creative papercraft demonstrate how this fascinating hobby can, with relatively little cost, absorb the whole family. Whether your choice is to make functional or purely decorative objects, I hope you will use the designs as a starting point to inspire your own individual ideas.

Pamela Woods

Paper cut-out designs are very simple to
make and give good practice in cutting
neatly and handling different textured
papers.

Types of Paper

There is an enormous range of different types of paper varying from tissue to card, or foil to cartridge, patterned and plain, textured and smooth. One can be constantly on the hunt for different patterns, textures and colours, and each new discovery inspires fresh ideas and new projects. Whether used on their own, or for wrapping or decorative purposes, there are endless combinations to interest a papercraft enthusiast. Choosing colours and patterns to enhance each other and the quality of the proposed project can be as rewarding and stimulating as actually making the object. The following may be helpful in choosing the most suitable paper for each project.

Card

This is a general term which covers a range of strawboards, cardboards, and mounting boards, the latter being paper mounted for display work. The material can, of course, be cut and scored and is suitable for constructional or display purposes. Card is the only strength of paper which is suitable for box-making. Some boards are already prepared for display purposes, others require covering either by loose wrapping, or by using a spray mounting solution which is specially made for the purpose.

Cartridge Paper

This stiff, fairly heavy paper is made for drawing and other art work. It is beautifully crisp to handle, and when used for paper sculpture the most subtle shadows appear on the clear white surfaces. It can be scored, cut, folded, curled, and rolled with precision, resulting in clear-cut craftwork. The strength of this paper can be used to support other relatively flimsy papers.

Art paper is a general title which covers all the white and coloured papers used for painting and drawing, which do not fall into any other specific category.

Cover Paper

This is a stiff type of cartridge paper which is available in a wide range of colours and several different weights. The colours have the advantage of being absorbed into the paper rather than printed onto it.

Its handling properties are similar to cartridge paper and it is often used to provide a strong backing for flimsier papers such as tissue and crepe.

Sugar Paper

This is a fairly close-textured paper of a similar weight to cartridge paper. It is used in many schools because it is not only relatively inexpensive, but there are many assorted colours available.

Ingres Paper

This is one of the finest art papers, which is produced in an extensive range of subtle colours. Being a flat paper, it will cut into curls, roll and fold, and wherever it is included in design work it can only enrich a product. It is perfect material for printing.

Japanese Handmade Papers

The Japanese people have been

master papermakers for hundreds of years, and their tradition of hand-made papers is still retained. Their masterly craft produces delicate and intricate papers, some of which have carefully retained fibres in their composition as part of their design. Whether including leaves and real butterflies, or straw and rice fibres, their hand-made papers are absolutely fascinating. There is a specialised selection of traditional Japanese lacy papers which are hand-made. Their formulae are family secrets which have passed through generations. They have fascinating names such as 'Kotobuki' which has a daisy pattern and 'Rakasui-Haña-As' which is perforated with stars.

Coloured Paper

There are some fine white papers which are coated on one side in a single colour. These can range from bright primary colours, either matt or shiny, to a brilliant range of fluorescent colours, or gentle, earthy colours. With a white reverse these papers need to be used double if they are to be viewed from both sides. This type of paper is ideal for bright poster work.

Flocked Paper

A very rich, velvet-textured paper is achieved by flocking a coloured ground. The unique texture of its rich surface enhances the shiny, matt, crinkled, plain or patterned surfaces of all the other papers, by contrasting with them. Naturally this paper is a heavy one but when used flat, coiled or undulating the light falling on its fluffy surface gives it visual interest.

Paper-backed Foil

This is the most widely used paper for Christmas decorations. A white paper backing is coated with foil on one side, and consequently is a strong double paper for coverings, packaging and three-dimensional craft work. Many

are supplied in bold, metallic colours on a roll, but it is possible to find sheets of eggshell finish as well as shiny foil papers. These come in subtle shades of pink, turquoise, bronze, copper, silver, gold and, of course, the primary colours. Variations within the materials, using assorted metallic colours, can create an intriguing effect of contrasting and reflecting textures.

Tissue Paper

The most flimsy of all papers, the featherweight quality of tissue makes it almost translucent. A special quality to be found in tissue is the intensity of colour which is enriched when several layers are put together. The shades are strong, bordering on the iridescent, and dazzling combinations can be made. It is possible to buy packets of assorted colours of tissue which is more economical than buying a packet of a single colour when mixing and combining colours. The only drawback is that tissue paper colours have a tendency to fade easily, but that should not deter the inclusion of tissue in papercraft.

Crepe Paper

This is a lightweight paper usually made in assorted bright colours. The entire paper is crinkled and derives its name from the French 'crêpe de Chine', a silk fabric which is also crinkled. In English the French spelling is retained, but in America it is spelt 'crape'. Being a flimsy paper, only small pieces support their weight, but the crinkles give extra support. Crepe paper is normally sold in a fold of approx. 50 cm (20 in) × 2·6 m (8 ft 6 in), or on a roll to buy by the metre. The former gives better protection as, naturally, it cannot be ironed if creased by mistake. This is one of the best papers to mould, as easing out the crinkles creates a bowl shape in the centre, or a frill at the edge. This is the ideal material for paper twine as the elasticity gives added strength and binds the twine together. Crepe paper is very good for rolling and curling.

This is one of the easier papers to sew, particularly with a machine. The texture makes folding and tearing irregular, but it will of course cut properly. It is probably one of the easiest papers to manipulate, and therefore is ideal for flower-making. For coarse crepe paper work it can be dampened and allowed to dry again as this will enlarge the crinkles. Interesting effects can be obtained by dampening two contrasting tones together to make the colours mingle.

Double Crepe Paper

This variation is composed of two layers of single crepe paper adhered to each other. It has all the qualities of single crepe, and can of course be handled in the same way. It can be bought in packeted folds. Often manufactured in two tones or colours, interesting effects emerge with designs which involve the use of both sides of the paper. Roses and lilies are perfect examples of flowers which can be made with curly petals revealing a contrasting colour. Being double it naturally has considerably more strength than the single variety, but used together they complement each other.

Foil Crepe Paper

As the name suggests this is a paper-backed foil, which is crinkled into crepe. The flexibility varies according to the backing paper; for example there is the very fine German foil crepe which is very light to handle, moulding at the slightest touch, whilst some of the heavier papers can take relatively firm handling. Available in the basic colours of red, green, blue, gold and silver, the German crepe has

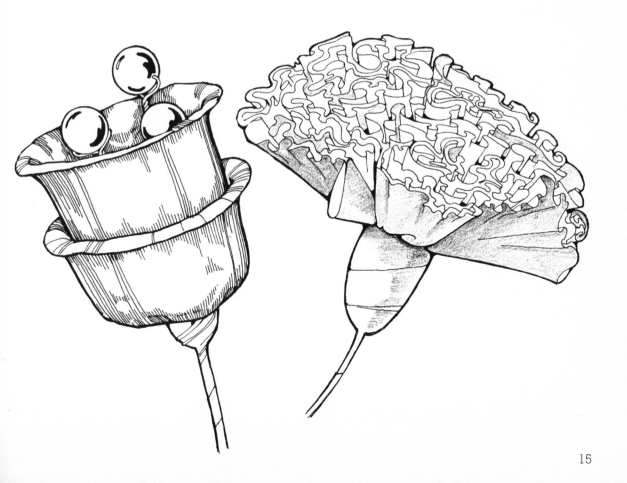

a white backing. The heavier crepe is made in subtle colours such as metallic bronze, green, lime, turquoise, silver, gold and others, but has a brown backing. The latter is obtainable by the metre, whilst the German is sold in packeted folds.

The backing is intended as such, and most probably should be covered by the same or other material. Expensive material like this can only reflect the quality in a design rather than create it. This textured foil is an excellent contrast to the flat metallic materials available for use in Christmas work. The handling properties are, naturally, the same as for all the other crepe papers.

Glass Crepe Paper

This delicate, translucent paper is actually crinkled cellophane. Whilst being ideal for decorative purposes, it is the texture which is fascinating, and can be used to emphasise other materials. If used on its own without backing material its transparency tends to make the edges ill-defined. So, for example, when it is used for a frill it should be used in combination with another crepe, which would enhance the cellophane qualities.

Cellophane and Acetate Film

The true form of cellophane, the brittle film used by the Victorians and early lantern slide operators is now generally replaced by P.V.C. film. It is generally transparent, and according to the density of colour may be used to change the colour of the object beneath. Light may be passed through it to create a coloured beam.

The P.V.A., or Acetate film, is produced as a clear film which is coated in colour, or silver, on one or both sides. Acetate foil sheeting is a springy and exciting reflective material to use, with various weights providing relative degrees of strength. Foil sheeting when plain, printed, or indeed patterned on one side is a variation of this material.

Wrapping Paper

Strictly speaking, any paper could be used for wrapping as a protective coating. However, wrapping paper is a name which has developed to cover all those decorative patterned papers which have been primarily produced for wrapping parcels. The markings on these have developed greatly from simple geometric patterns to elaborate designs which are worthy of being displayed on the wall as pictures. Nothing is more rewarding than a visit to a paper shop whose shelves are packed with an array of inviting wrapping papers.

Wall and Drawer Papers

There is a vast scope for the artist, or interior designer, in creating patterns for wall and drawer paper. This provides yet another enormous range of patterns and textures for the papercraft worker.

Additional Materials

There is a traditional saying that a bad workman blames his tools, and the easiest way to combat this is to be well prepared for the work before starting. There seems little need to stress the importance of keeping cutting tools sharp, having a work surface on which to cut, the correct glue for the job and a receptacle in which to hold it. This is important with free-flowing varieties where a gentle squeeze of the tube in a fresh position will draw the glue back in again, and prevent dripping.

Adhesives

Uhu is one of the best of all-purpose, clear, impact adhesives, but care is needed when using P.V.A. or polystyrene as it tends to dissolve them. Pritt is another useful all-purpose glue, however almost any impact adhesive is suitable for papercraft.

Other forms of fixative such as the various adhesive tapes are so useful it is hard to imagine papercraft without them. A stapler, too, is a machine which is being used increasingly in paperwork.

Apart from the usual methods of joining, there are times when quantities are assembled by tying together with string, cord, tape, or ribbon. These materials, as well as chenille wire, feathers, lace, beads, sequins and glitter, to name but a few, can contribute towards collage or emphasise a contrasting material on three-dimensional work.

Cutting Tools

Scissors are obviously essential for work with paper, as is a sharp knife. A Stanley knife with removable blades is suitable for cutting thick card whereas a lighter knife is useful for thinner papers. It is essential to use a good knife for scoring and precise cutting.

Equipment for Making Flowers

Basic essentials for flower-making are stem and binding wires, and binding tape, although crepe paper cut into strips makes an adequate substitute for the latter. Beads and sequins are also useful for flowerwork, as, too, are various dried plant materials. The solid, and somewhat simple, appearance of paper flowers may be relieved by the intricate delicacy of dried plants, particularly as stamens in the centre of paper petals.

Pens, Pencils and Paint

Many patterned papers require no further decoration. However some papercraft requires plain paper with certain markings, and there is a variety of media suitable for this. Various paints are applied wet but some, such as chalks, pencils and pastilles are used dry. These have the disadvantage of smudging when handled frequently. This type of marking can be controlled with ease although it is not always sufficiently strong and needs a certain degree of pressure for its application. This is not always possible on a delicately constructed object.

Pencils are ideal for measuring out patterns since they can be easily erased. For measuring purposes a ruler, tape measure, compasses and eraser are also necessary.

Water colours and designers' colours are useful for pattern making of all kinds, provided the surface to be

Choose a pleasant place to work with a
good, flat table top, if possible near a
source of natural light.

1 Cover paper
2 Transparent acetate film
3 Glass crepe paper
4 Paper-backed foil with textured finish
5 Paper-backed foil
6 Foil crepe paper
7 Coloured card
8 Flocked paper
9 Hand-made Japanese paper
10 Two-tone double crepe paper
11 Wrapping paper
12 Tissue paper
13 Miniature doyleys

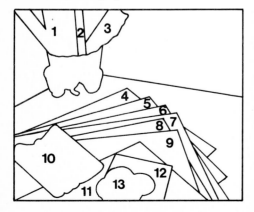

coated is absorbent. The intensity of the colour can be easily controlled by adding water, and a variety of marks from the tiniest pin prick, to complete colour washes can be created with the use of a variety of brushes.

There are some materials, such as shiny, coloured card, which have a non-absorbent surface and therefore require paints such as acrylic, or oil colour, which are not water based. Out of the two, acrylic is the most adaptable medium to use: it can be diluted with water or used straight from the tube.

This paint has the additional quality of being extremely fast drying and a certain amount of interesting three-dimensional work can be produced by building the surface of the paint into wrinkles, peaks and hollows. These

textures can be created with conventional brushwork or with a palette knife. Designers' colours can be mixed with cryla media and then used in the same way. This gives the substance of the paint considerable strength, and it can be indented by printing with firm objects. These provide subtle variations to the surface and give interesting textures to animals and plants.

For use in collage work the acrylic media has the dual qualities of colouring and adhesion. So immediately the area receives a coating of colour the additional material can be embedded directly into the paint. Cryla media can be used on its own or mixed with paint, but if used alone it dries transparent

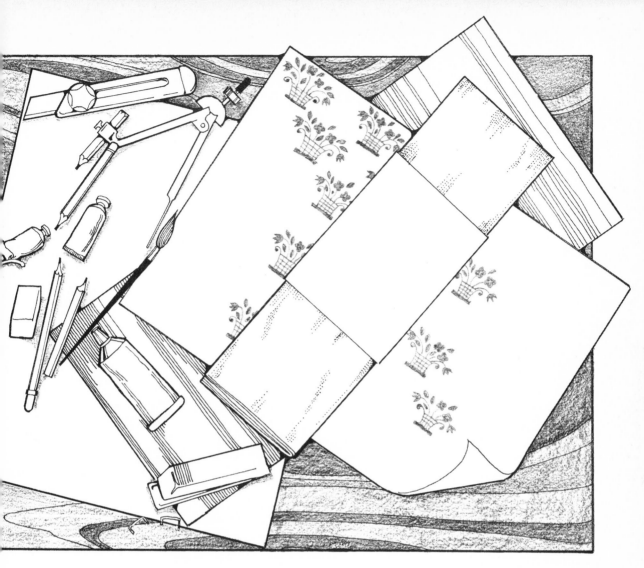

and is, therefore, not only a glue but a good sealing coat for a working surface. Not to be confused with a varnish, which is to provide a finish, this material is a surface medium which is an essential ingredient for craft work.

Varnish

There are two main types of varnish: matt or glossy, and they can be either painted over the surface or sprayed from an aerosol can. This second form of application is the most adaptable for three-dimensional craft work as it provides a thin film of varnish which coats the object without the distortion which is difficult to avoid under the pressure of a brush.

Découpage is a process which has developed over the years. Originally a Victorian craft, it is the application of several layers of varnish. The aim of the process is to apply a picture or pattern to an object like a wooden box, a mirror, a glass, or a tin box, and then by the careful repetitive process of sandpapering and recoating several layers of varnish, to develop a shiny, level surface where the edge of the applied picture is undetectable. Patterns like those in a scrapbook can be built up and arrangements of flowers, cut from old greetings cards and wrapping paper, can be applied layer upon layer to produce interesting effects.

With a well-equipped work table there is every possibility of good results.

1 Valentine card
2 Mother's Day card
3 Christmas card
4 Birthday card
5 Pop-up card
6 Easter card

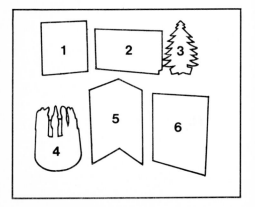

Dried plant materials
combine well with paper
to make unusual flowers and
garlands. See page 141 for detailed
instructions.

24

— Techniques of Paper Handling —

A flat piece of paper to the craftsman is the same as a blank canvas to the artist, a terrific invitation which holds a lot of potential. Thankfully, an artist is never so completely satisfied with his last work that he is not fired with enthusiasm to start the next: the craftsman is the same.

To create three-dimensional objects, the paper needs to be shaped, and there are various ways of doing this. To create flat, plain shapes the paper is folded or pleated. This can be simple, or complicated as in some origami patterns.

Some papers do not lend themselves to this form of manipulation, owing to their stiffness, but with the help of scoring, dips and hollows can be created. Scoring is making a line with a knife which half cuts into the paper, thus making folding easier. Straight or curved lines can be used to make intriguing shapes.

For a more rounded effect which allows the surface to attract or reflect the light, the paper can be rolled or coiled, or pulled over a knife to produce a curl or tight coil. Scissors and knives obviously play an important part in shaping, or cutting paper. Punched holes can be put to effective decorative use.

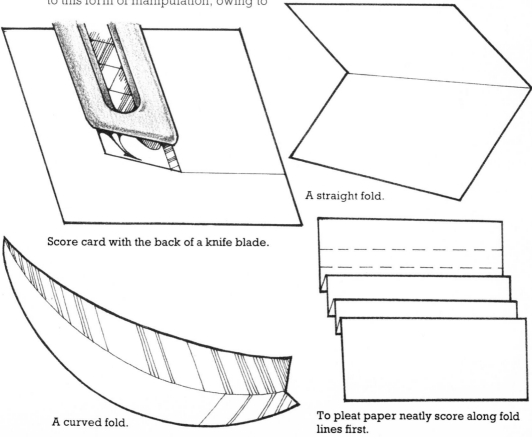

A straight fold.

Score card with the back of a knife blade.

A curved fold.

To pleat paper neatly score along fold lines first.

The Advent Calendar and a Scrap Book –
two fascinating ways of putting old
Christmas and birthday cards to good use.

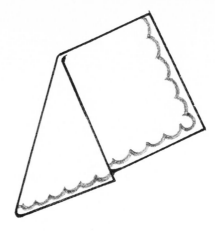

Practise folding using paper table napkins. For the cone, first fold the napkin in half.

Bring the upper corners down from the fold to form the cone shape.

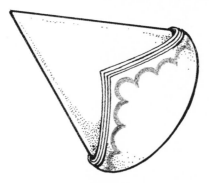

Crepe Paper

Crepe paper has a special quality of its own because of the wrinkles. Various shapes are created by easing these out so that the flat area is larger than the creased one. This is most clearly shown when the creases are eased out at the edge, as this will produce a frill. However, if the shaping is made in the centre of a piece of crepe paper the creases on each side will enclose the stretched area, so that a cup or dome shape will appear. In the same way that a cup or dome shape is made, a double curve can be produced by stretching the creases close to each other on opposite sides of the paper; this shape is particularly suitable for flower petals. Thin strips of crepe paper, when stretched diagonally across the creases into a tube shape, will, by reason of its pliability, retain a tight twisted twine appearance. This twine is surprisingly strong compared with the flat paper, and being

Fold up the point to hold the shape and provide a level base.

increased in flexibility it is very versatile and can be knotted, twisted, crocheted, woven, and even knitted.

It is not always easy to paint crepe paper, particularly with water-based colours, but by simply using water special effects can be achieved. For example, two varying shades of crepe paper can be folded together and dipped into water until the material has absorbed sufficient moisture, then squeezed gently and left to dry. It is not essential to use varying colours as single colours work perfectly well, but it is interesting to achieve blending and colour integration by this method. This will have a discolouring effect which can create a light pattern on a dark surface.

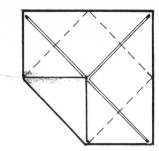

Open the napkin out flat and fold all corners to the centre. Repeat this process twice.

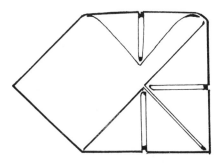

Turn the napkin over and fold points to the centre on the other side.

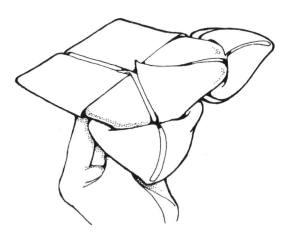

Turn again and holding all the points together in the centre gently pull down the two layers of petals to form a lily shape.

Quilling

Quilling, is a craft which, being a particular favourite of the Victorians, is now enjoying popularity in America. The process is basically very simple, and is achieved by rolling thin strips of paper round a stick the size of a cocktail stick. Lightweight single layered paper is the most satisfactory for quilling, as the shapes must hold themselves; however even tissue paper is suitable. There are various shapes which can be made to contribute to a varied pattern, from curls, tight and loose rolls, to scrolls, hearts and 'S' shapes. The approximate dimensions of each strip are 0·5 cm ($\frac{1}{4}$ in) × 20 cm (8 in), but will vary with specific requirements.

To make the tight roll:—
Hold the strip firmly to the side of the quilling stick and rotate it so that the paper rolls round it, making sure that the paper stays at the same level and does not spiral down the stick (Fig. 1). Secure with glue and carefully remove the roll, keeping it intact.

To make the loose roll:—
Prepare the strip of paper in the same way as for the tight roll, and then allow it to spring open, but be ready with the glue to secure it at the right size. If there are several loose curls required to be exactly the same size it is a good idea to find something to hold the shape in, like a small lid, or to make one by cutting a hole in two layers of card and sticking them together. If the centre of the roll opens out so far that the spiral is not visible it may be necessary to squeeze the roll before it is allowed to spring open. The loose roll can be pinched in one or more places to produce crescent, dewdrop, pointed oval, triangular or other shapes.

To make a curl:—
Make a tight roll and secure the end, and then allow the paper to slip as it is removed from the stick to produce a long spiral (Fig. 2).

1 Small gusseted carrier bag
2 Curved bag
3 Cylindrical parcel
4 Hexagonal box
5 Triangular box
6 Novelty box in the shape of an owl
7 Large gusseted carrier bag
8 Parcel wrapped in napkins
9 Plain carrier bag
10 Doyley bag
11 Parcel decorated with tissue flowers
12 Cylinder decoratively wrapped
13 Decorated papier mâché egg

Some of the great variety of ways of
presenting gifts to your family and friends.

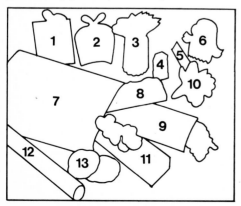

To make a scroll:—

Start rolling the strip of paper as for the previous shapes, but work only as far as the centre of the strip. Squeeze the roll and allow it to spring open, and remove the stick. This will produce an open-ended shape. Repeat the process from the other side of the paper leaving the curls touching in the middle (Fig. 3).

To make a heart:—

This is the same as the scroll shape, but the flat centre point is pinched to form a point (Fig. 4).

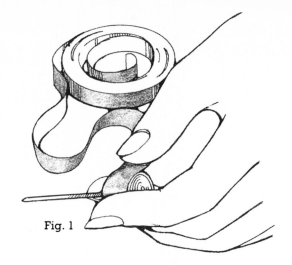

Fig. 1

To make the 'S' shape:—

Make the first part of the scroll, and then the second working the paper the opposite way (Fig. 5).

Apart from those shapes made with the stick there are some others which will add to the variety. The strips can be carefully plaited, or folded into a zig-zag concertina shape. Both these shapes are particularly useful, not only as a contrast to the others, but the lines can be used to contain or join areas of solid quilling. It is possible to produce shapes such as the scroll, and other open-ended shapes by pulling the paper over a knife but whilst this can be perfectly satisfactory it is not always easy to control, particularly in fine work.

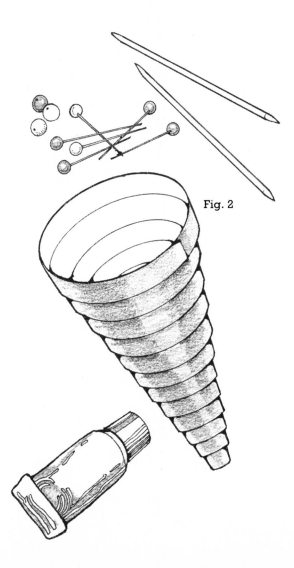

Fig. 2

Uses for Quilled Paper

These are the traditional quilling shapes which are made with a quilling stick and are applied to a flat surface with glue.

There are, of course, numerous designs which can be made with a combination of various quills. One of the favourites of the Victorians was a coat-of-arms. They would encrust these sophisticated, geometric designs with tiny jewels and paint the surface of the quills with metallic paint to emphasise the detail of the spirals.

Although traditionally quilling is a flat form of collage or decoration it is also possible to use the craft for three-dimensional work. The patterns are

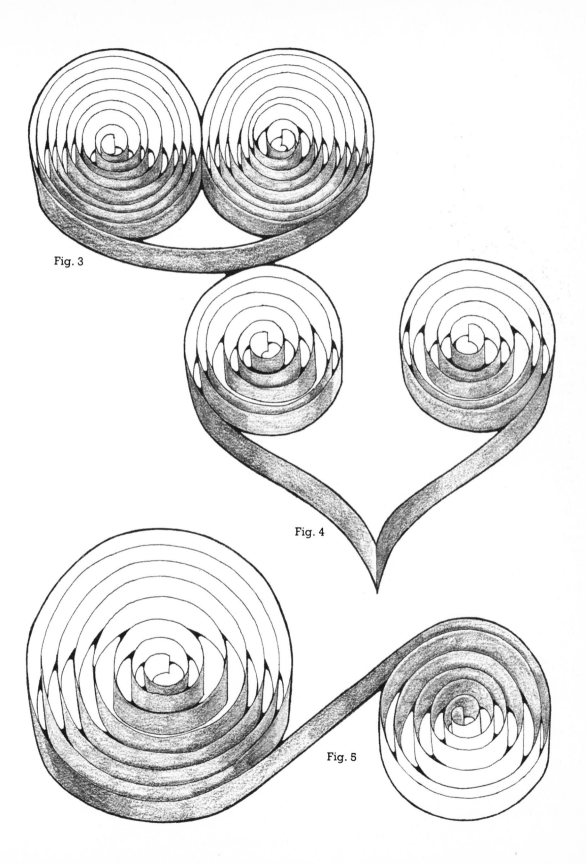

Fig. 3

Fig. 4

Fig. 5

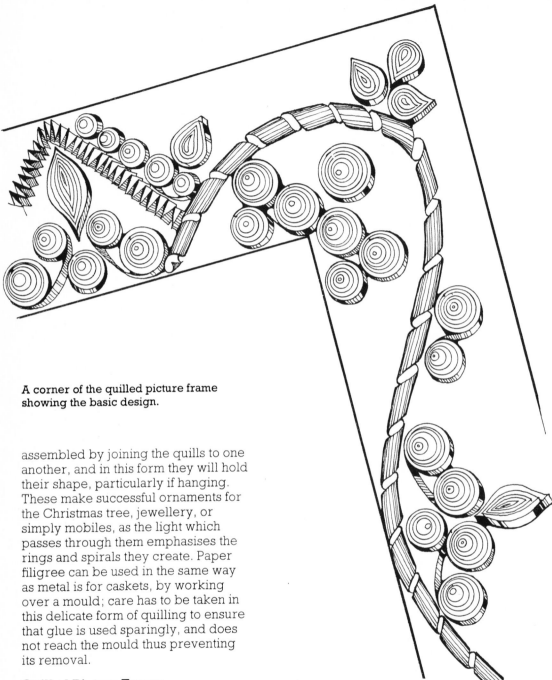

A corner of the quilled picture frame showing the basic design.

assembled by joining the quills to one another, and in this form they will hold their shape, particularly if hanging. These make successful ornaments for the Christmas tree, jewellery, or simply mobiles, as the light which passes through them emphasises the rings and spirals they create. Paper filigree can be used in the same way as metal is for caskets, by working over a mould; care has to be taken in this delicate form of quilling to ensure that glue is used sparingly, and does not reach the mould thus preventing its removal.

Quilled Picture Frame

This shows an easy and attractive idea for practising quilling techniques. Mount a favourite postcard, picture or even photograph in a broad card frame and then decorate with assorted quills, using papers which reflect the colours in the picture. Most thin papers are suitable for this as long as they are single layered, since double papers often come apart in the rolling process. The emphasis of the design is, in fact, put on the contrast between loose and tight curls and the whole pattern is interlinked with long curls and concertina folded paper. The whole of this design may be produced using an ordinary cocktail stick for curling.

Papier-mâché

Papier-mâché is another ancient craft which is still continued today in Thailand, where nimble fingers and fine artistry produce intricately decorated boxes. As the name suggests, the paper is reduced to a pulp either by being mixed with a water and flour paste, or used in thin layers of tiny pieces each applied with the paste. As the paste seeps through, the saturated paper is built up to form an even coating over a mould. The surface of the mould, e.g. thimbles, eggs, bowls, boxes and balloons must first be coated with some grease or butter. Then, when sufficient layers have been built up, it should be left to dry thoroughly and carefully eased off the mould. In the case of the egg or any other spherical shape, where the mould is entirely coated, it is necessary to cut through the papier-mâché so that it can be taken away in two halves. The balloon, however, can simply be popped, an operation which is always undertaken with some trepidation.

Interesting effects can be produced with tissue paper, where a thin coating of layers is applied: when the balloon is removed, the delicate sphere can be used as a translucent lampshade, where the light emphasises the various overlapping layers.

Decorated Easter Eggs

Two papercraft techniques: papier mâché and découpage are here combined to produce this delightful Easter egg.

Form the papier mâché egg round a greased mould using strips of tissue paper and a stiff flour and water paste (Fig. 1). Allow to dry overnight before removing from the mould. When completely dry coat with acrylic gesso which is sold for this purpose in craft shops. A thick acrylic paint would serve almost as well and gives the egg a lovely bright covering. This enhances any patterns which you

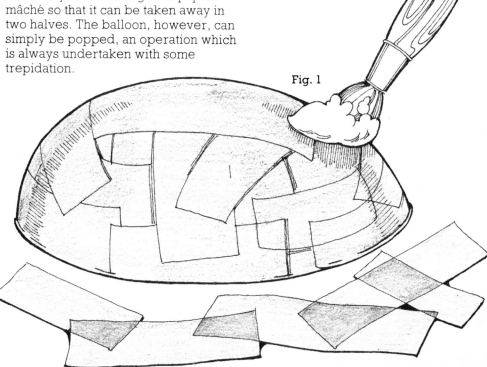

Fig. 1

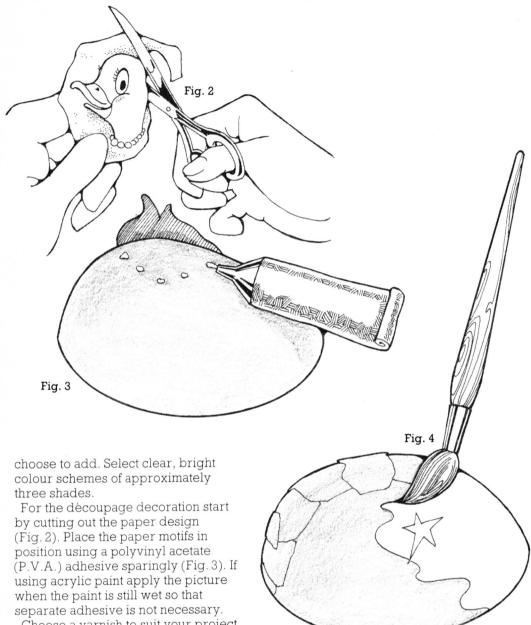

Fig. 2

Fig. 3

Fig. 4

choose to add. Select clear, bright colour schemes of approximately three shades.

For the découpage decoration start by cutting out the paper design (Fig. 2). Place the paper motifs in position using a polyvinyl acetate (P.V.A.) adhesive sparingly (Fig. 3). If using acrylic paint apply the picture when the paint is still wet so that separate adhesive is not necessary.

Choose a varnish to suit your project. Thick, slower drying varnish tends to give a very durable finish but lacquer based varnish, available in spray form will give quicker results. Apply the varnish with smooth even strokes, starting at the centre (Fig. 4), stroking very lightly at the edges where it tends to build up.

After approximately fifteen layers of varnish, when the edges of the paper no longer stand out from the surface,

use sandpaper and fine wire wool to make the surface absolutely smooth. This may be repeated until you are absolutely satisfied with the surface.

Finally wipe the surface with a damp, soapy cloth and buff up with a dry cloth.

36

Greetings Cards

Greetings cards need not always be created by artists, although their expertise can never be matched. There are many aspects of papercraft which can be employed and with the use of some exotic papers and various ways of cutting and marking attractive cards can be made.

Again, reference should be made to the Victorians and their ingenious use of paper, as the exchanging of Christmas cards was a custom which was only begun in their day. The original cards were very simple: painted writing paper, illustrated greetings, or packaged paintings. The introduction of the penny post in 1840 did much to encourage the exchange of these charming forms of greeting.

The Valentine card was even more popular than the Christmas card with the Victorians and developed from the elaborate forms of New Year greetings they used to send. Highly decorated, with all manner of lace, ribbons and pictures to enhance their messages, some of those beautiful cards are still being imitated today. With the pressure of time the present day designs tend to be slick, funny or basically very simple, their significance is, however, the same.

The manufacture of greetings cards is such a commercial success today that it is quite amazing to learn that the very first commercially made Christmas card by Henry Cole, the founder of the Victoria & Albert Museum, was a failure! At all times of the year, whether it is Christmas, Easter, a birthday or a wedding, there are many reasons for the exchange of cards. There are even days in which the card seems to be the most important element, like Mothering Sunday and Valentine's Day, when feelings are portrayed by a message within the card.

Valentine Card

Typical of the Valentine card is the heart, a symbol of love, which can be decorated, padded or edged with lace. Ornamented with bows or ribbon, and maybe some paper doyleys, these cards are made by building up contrasting layers, each one to enhance the next. It is possible to find heart-shaped scraps, which could be incorporated into the design. In fact, the Valentine card can be an extravaganza of assorted layers of decoration.

This one is made from stiff silver foil card, with a heart-shaped card on the top followed by a flocked paper heart edged with a pleated strip from the edge of a paper doyley. The padded heart is a piece of crepe paper stretched over a cardboard heart, with a little cottonwool stuffing. Edged with another paper doyley, silver this time, the heart is finally decorated with a scrap. A padded heart of this kind is the perfect position for a secret message.

Pop-Up Card

The image on a card should essentially be a simple one as each card is a complete pictorial statement of a certain message.

A favourite amongst children is the cheerful pop-up card with the surprise moving centre which appears to greet the recipient. The clown is an example of this type and the contrasting colours show clearly the need for two layers where the outer casing forms a backing to the opening parts. All

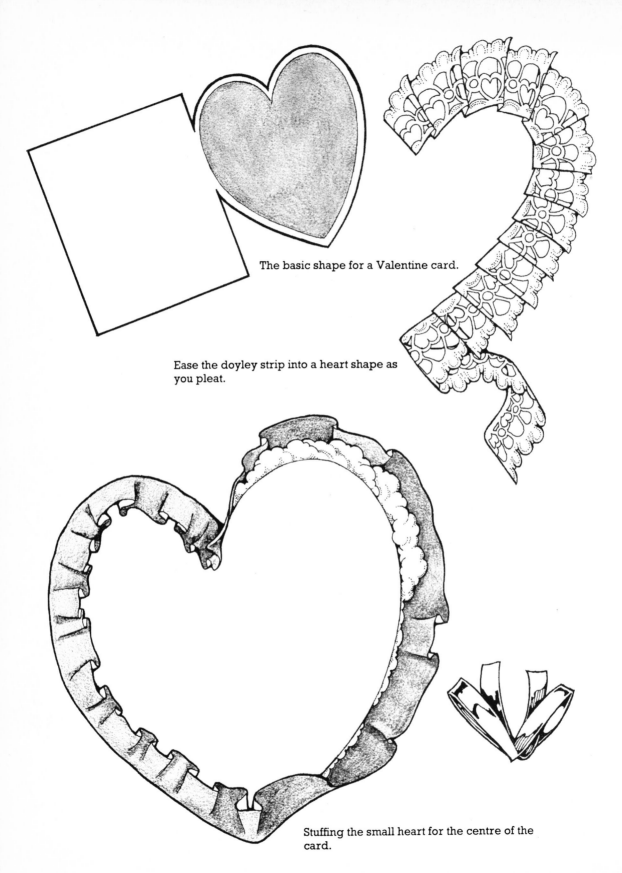

The basic shape for a Valentine card.

Ease the doyley strip into a heart shape as you pleat.

Stuffing the small heart for the centre of the card.

Fig. 1

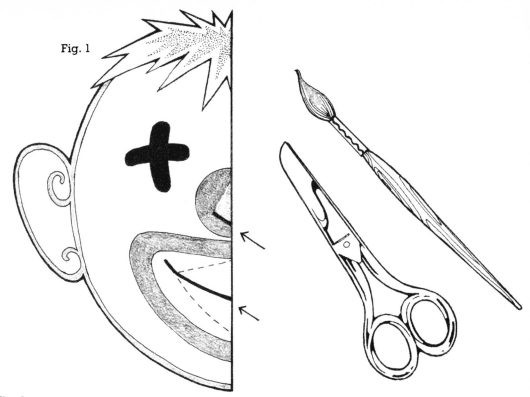

Fig. 2

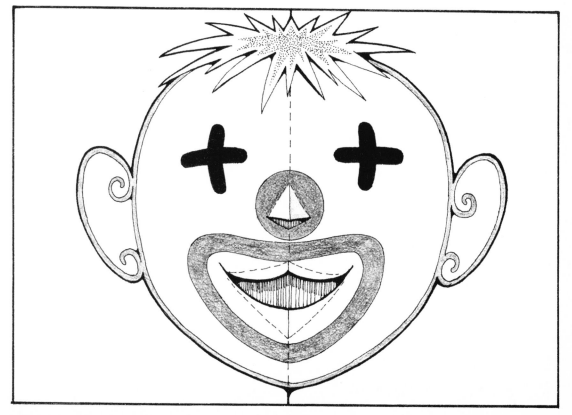

manner of varying shapes can be invented but the basic process is the same.

First paint a simple, bold face onto paper and fold it in half. Make a diagonal cut into the fold at the mouth (Fig. 1). Open out the face and invert the mouth piece at the fold line (Fig. 2).

Stick the face to the backing card. You will find on opening the card that the mouth will open and close. The idea of moving mouth or beak can be used for many humorous characters.

Mother's Day Card

This Mother's Day card is very simple to make. The letters are formed from strips of coloured paper. These are given a thin coating of glue along one edge, placed carefully onto the card and held in place until the glue is dry.

The card is decorated with little heart-shaped pieces which can be cut from scraps of wallpaper or wrapping paper and finished with curled strips of paper the same colour as the lettering.

Birthday Card

The birthday cake plays an important part in birthday celebrations and is represented by this unusual card.

It is made of a long strip of coloured card, 10 cm (4 in) × 50 cm (20 in), although the size can be varied as desired.

The frills are made from two strips of crepe paper the same length as the piece of card and 2·5 cm (1 in) wide. Frill the edges of the crepe along one side and stick inside the card at the top and bottom.

Cover the outside of the card with paper-backed foil or similar bright paper leaving the coloured edges showing. Paint on the birthday message (Fig. 1).

Make candles from pieces of rolled cartridge paper 8 cm (3 in) × 6·5 cm (2½ in) and top these off with 'flames' made from pointed oval shapes of crepe paper (Fig. 2) 6·5 cm (2½ in) × 2·5 cm (1 in) at the widest point.

Stick or staple the ends together to form a circular cake shape. This design leaves a liberal amount of space inside for writing messages.

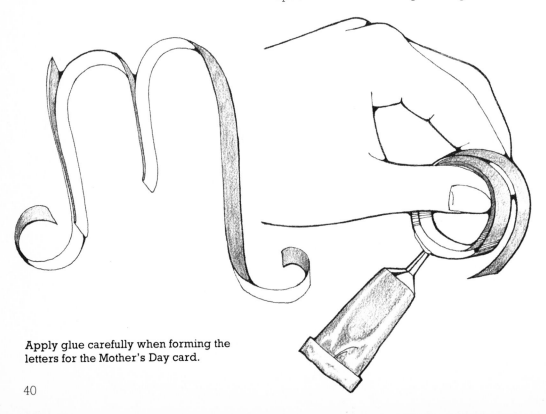

Apply glue carefully when forming the letters for the Mother's Day card.

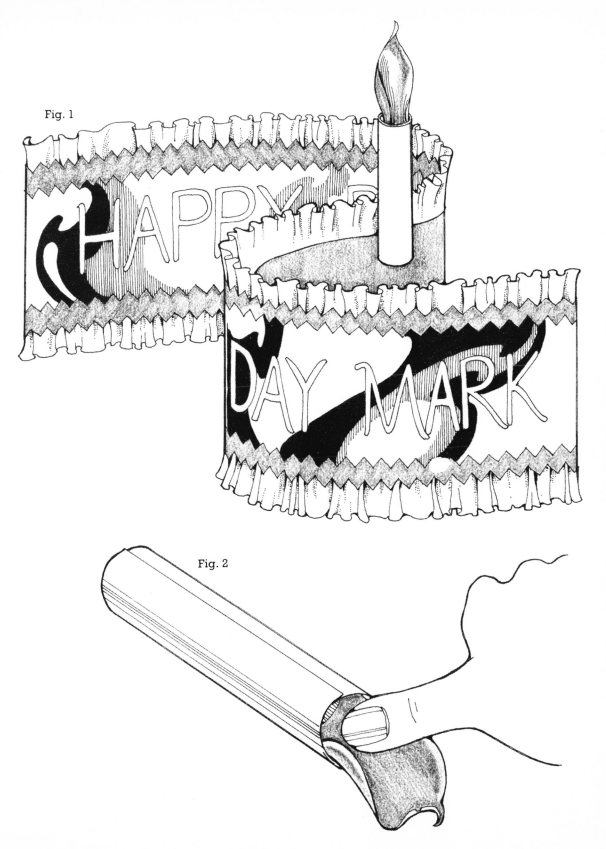

Fig. 1

HAPPY

DAY MARK

Fig. 2

41

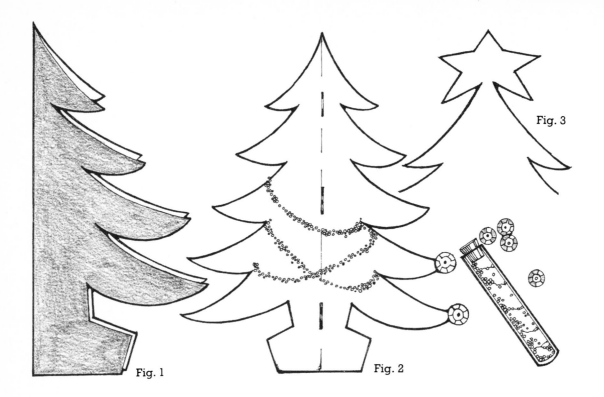

Fig. 3

Fig. 1

Fig. 2

Christmas Card

The commercial Christmas card is becoming more and more elaborate and the variety within the general theme increasing. The simple Christmas tree, easily recognisable, is chosen as the shape for this six page card.

Cut three identical Christmas tree shapes from green card and fold each one down the centre (Fig. 1). These should have a wide base to stand the card on.

Open them out again, lay them on top of one another and staple down the fold (Fig. 2), taking care not to staple away from the centre line as this would make opening the card out difficult. Finally open out the layers to radiate evenly and decorate as desired with paint, glitter or sequins.

A further variation on this card is to cut a star shape at the top of the tree (Fig. 3). When the tree is assembled this will form a three-dimensional pointed star.

Easter Card

This is a more conventional design. The chicken is made from small, pointed and cupped pieces of yellow crepe paper 2·5 cm (1 in) long. His eye and beak are rolled orange crepe paper which has been knotted for the eye and folded in half for the beak.

The broken egg is simply cut from cartridge paper. The bold white shape is enhanced by the blue background as are the white lines and lettering.

The Scrap Book

There are many papercraft customs for which we have the Victorians to thank, but perhaps the most charming of them all, and one which portrays their enthusiasm for collecting things, is scrap book making. They used all manner of pictures to fill their books which they went to elaborate lengths to make. In Cassell's Household Guide of 1877 the instructions on how to make a scrap book read:—

"Get a strong set of cards, of whatever size you like, they may be as much as twelve inches square. Lance holes with a penknife at each of the corners, and run a piece of coloured ribbon through after the fashion of a fan, having first bound the edges all round with ribbon put on with a strong solution of gum. Fig. 1 shows the manner of doing this. (The pictures will be placed in a long line.) After gumming down the ribbon, the cards not being more than the least possible space apart, leave them spread upon a table, covered with clean paper, and press them under a heavy weight. The next day the gum will be dry. One or more pictures can be arranged on each side of every card, and the covers may be ornamented with silk or moire antique, sewn together at the edges and put on after the ribbon joints. The merit of this book is that it will open like a common book either way, back and front, or unfold like a panorama."

This was just one of the shapes they suggested but more conventional books could also be made. There was always much emphasis on using elaborate fabric or embossed paper covering for a special collection. The contents varied from little keepsakes, like the love messages they received inside Christmas crackers, and equally sentimental messages portrayed within greetings cards, to cards which manufacturers inserted into their packages of cigarettes, tobacco, tea and other products.

These were intended as collectors' pictures and acquiring sets became an intriguing pastime which far outlived the original cards. All manner of subjects were portrayed in these little cards, which usually had a picture on the front and the back filled with information. There were many subjects from plants, people, events, geographical topics, to buildings, vehicles and astrology, so that the little cards had much to offer from an educational point of view.

As well as these, patterns cut from greetings cards, especially at Christmas time, provided material for keen scrap book creators. Picture cut-outs and little images were produced especially for the purpose and acquired the name of scraps. With this wealth of material the scrap books became treasuries of amassed memories, with layers of pictures which lifted up to reveal tiny images below.

The scrap book on page 27 was made for my own children. Each figure was cut from old Christmas cards, with a different Christmas subject on each page. There is a page made with rows of little houses which lift to reveal their occupants.

A charming thought, when the scrap book was made, was the addition in the back of some blank pages, together with some uncut cards, blunt scissors and glue, for the children to continue the book for themselves, so discovering the joys of making their own pages.

Fig. 1

The Advent Calendar

The Advent calendar is not only fun to make, but helps to increase the building excitement of the approach of Christmas. Each day a tiny door is opened until the day arrives when all the doors are open and all the contents are clearly visible. Although they appear intricate they are really not difficult to make.

Pierce the corner of each door with a point which penetrates the sheet below, this will ensure that the pictures are aligned in the correct position when the doors are opened. With the addition of glitter powder and extra scraps, the making of an Advent calendar can be as rewarding as watching the anticipation on the children's faces as they open the doors. Figures cut from old Christmas cards are ideal for this purpose.

First make the basic picture using clear, bold shapes cut from cover paper or card. This can be decorated later with a profusion of little figures, stars, glitter etc.

Mark and cut windows on the top picture. There should be twenty-five in all – one for each day from December 1st to Christmas Day. Use your imagination to find unusual places to cut them such as in the curve of the moon in this illustration.

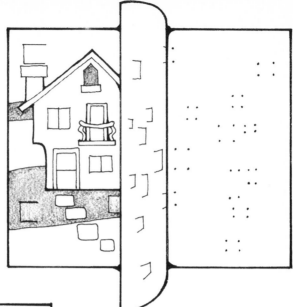

Place the top picture over a stiff card backing and use a pin to prick through the four corners of each door.

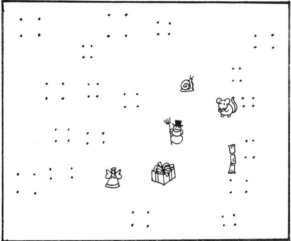

Use these marks to position assorted little figures and scraps so that they will be visible when the doors are opened.

When all the spaces have been filled the top sheet can be stuck over the backing board. Care must be taken to ensure that none of the doors are accidentally stuck down. It is traditional to number the doors from one to twenty-five, but it is not necessary as long as the special large door for Christmas Day itself is made obvious.

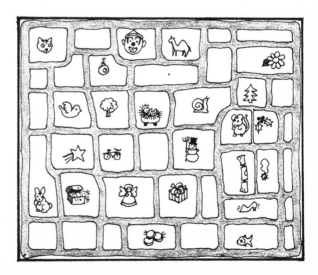

Gift Tags

Gift tags are useful attached to a present either as a substitute for a card or in addition to one. They can be made in many shapes and sizes, from plain or coloured card or stiff paper. Use motifs cut from magazines or Christmas cards or ready cut and gummed shapes such as paper stars. Alternatively use paints and felt tip pens and make your own design. The illustrations below will give you some idea of the wide range of possibilities.

Gift Wrapping

Parcels

The anticipation of an unopened parcel has a special thrill of its own, the wrapping material concealing the contents from the receiver. A disguising wrapping can add to the enthusiasm to reveal the contents. Whether an absolutely plain brown parcel paper appearing through the post, or the most elaborately decorated object, the fact that someone has taken the trouble to wrap an object before sending or giving it, deserves gratitude.

There are special requirements for parcels which have to withstand the hardships of transport, and time invested in providing adequately strong wrapping materials can only increase the safety of the contents in transit. Plain paper, allowing positive writing to clarify the destination, strong string to tie the parcel together and, if necessary, a box to protect fragile contents are essential for all postal wrapping. However if the parcel is to be handed to the recipient in the form of a gift then decorative wrapping can have elaborate attention to emphasise the fact that the contents are a gift.

Wrapping a Box

The simplest of all shapes to wrap is a box, and many manufacturers provide their merchandise in most elaborate packaging. However, even these deserve the disguise of an outer coating. There are numerous decorative wrapping papers designed by artists especially for the purpose, and a sheet of one of these wrapped and folded round the box and tied with toning cord or ribbon is an effective, if simple, form of gift wrapping. There may be a little spare paper left over and a variation on the ribbon decoration would be a spray of little flowers using up the pieces. If plain paper is also available, as on page 30 brown tissue, then the spray can be enhanced by a few plain flowers.

Using Table Napkins

Time may not allow a second trip to the shops so a hunt round the house may provide some suitable wrapping paper. Some paper table napkins in various shades can be used for a soft wrapping, and here two toning colours have been combined to wrap a box. The little decorations on the top are made by folding the napkin into four and cutting a little disc 2·5 cm (1 in) across through all the layers at once.

This is repeated with the second napkin in the other colour and the two are threaded together with a short piece of wire. Rub the sides of the discs to separate the layers to form the shaping in the centre. The two decorations here emphasise the second colour of the napkin, visible only in the centre.

Wrapping a Cylinder

Cylindrical shapes appear often in commercial packaging and present their own wrapping problems. However, the curved surface enhances the design on most wrapping paper and certainly improves foil and other reflective papers. The addition of a plain paper cut-out design round the base of the cylinder outlines one of the ends and gives visual weight to the base of the parcel.

If a sophisticated but plain cylindrical wrapping for a man is required, then this folded brown paper one may be suitable. The paper is cut so that it is the same width as the height of the cylinder and then marked along both sides at 2·5 cm (1 in) and 1 cm ($\frac{1}{2}$ in) alternatively. Use the marks as guides to making concertina folds all along the paper, these will open out slightly when it is curved round the cylinder. The sharp line at the end of the parcel is relieved by the fan of pleated tissue paper which echoes the pleats on the parcel.

Wrapping a Sphere

It is almost impossible to disguise a sphere and this can ruin the element of surprise which is the purpose of gift wrapping. The two ideas here have been chosen for a man and a woman – it is obvious which is which!

Tissue Flower

To wrap a ball as a tissue flower first cover the ball in a double layer of tissue. Then cut eight rounded petal discs from two toning colours of tissue paper (Fig. 1). Thread these onto a piece of wire and twist this round at the back to secure the layers (Fig. 2). Rotate the layers to allow as many as possible to be visible.

Dab glue at a few random points to stop the layers separating altogether. Make a ring of glue on the flower and wrap it round the covered ball.

Hat

To make the hat cut a long strip of black cover paper so that it encircles the ball and stands a little taller than it when fixed into a ring. Place the ball inside and put the two on top of a large disc which will form the brim.

Cut a second disc slightly larger than the crown and score an inner circle to fit the inside of the ring. Cut into it all round the edge to form tabs. Apply glue to them all and fix them inside the ring (Fig. 3). At this stage also secure the brim to the crown. The finishing touch is the strip of grey paper added as a hat band.

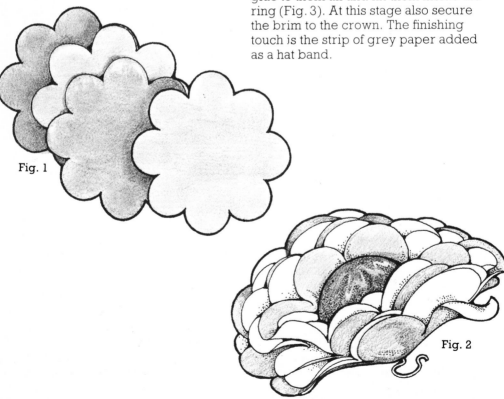

Fig. 1

Fig. 2

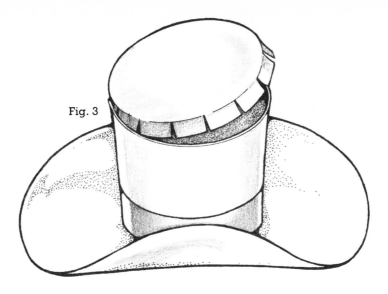

Fig. 3

Decorative Bags

Plain

Many soft and light gifts require a delicate form of packaging, and there are decorative bags of all kinds available in the shops. These are very simple to make with wrapping paper, wallpaper or plain paper of sufficient strength, and homemade bags have the added advantage of being tailor-made for the gift. Whatever the size or proportion the process is the same: first cut a rectangular piece of paper and fold one of the longest sides down 2·5 cm (1 in) to form the top (Fig. 1). Fold the paper almost in half across the width so that a small strip is allowed at the side (Fig. 2). Fold this inside, and secure it with glue. This

stage produces a flat tube with one side folded in.

To make the base fold the tube at the raw edge up 4 cm (1½ in) (Fig. 3), then separate the layers, open them out and press flat to form a point on either side (Fig. 4). Next fold the lower fold up across the fold line (Fig. 5), and then fold the upper one down in the same way so that they overlap, and secure this with glue (Fig. 6). This last series of folds is the vital part which forms the bag. Finally make two holes in the top and thread a piece of ribbon or cord through them. When the glue is dry the bag can be opened out in the normal way.

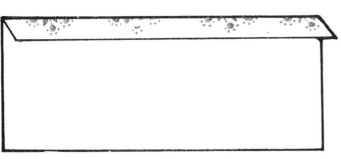

Fig. 1

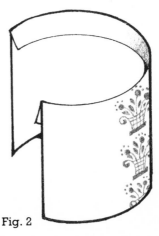

Fig. 2

Fig. 3

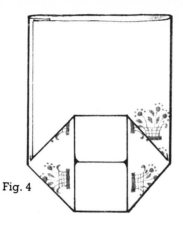

Fig. 4

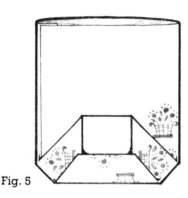

Fig. 5

Fig. 6

Gusseted Bag

To make a gusseted bag, which is a more sophisticated version of the conventional carrier bag, the top fold is made in exactly the same way, and the tube is joined as before. Then make an inward fold of the bag on either side 2·5 cm (1 in) (Fig. 1), and

fold the base of raw edges up 5 cm (2 in). Open the layers out and press the point at which the gusset meets the fold (Fig. 2). Press the sides flat and complete the envelope fold by the same process as the carrier bag (Fig. 3). This shape of bag is particularly suitable for homemade sweets, especially when special papers are used.

Fig. 1

Fig. 2

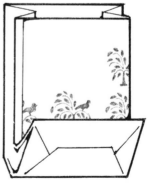

Fig. 3

Curved Bag

Thirdly, a variation on the paper bag can be made with a curved base and a curved top to echo this. This one is easy to assemble as it is simply fixed together with one flap inside another. Follow the cutting pattern (Fig. 1), scoring the dotted lines and assemble (Fig. 2). It is felt that to fold the top on a curved edge would result in a clumsy finish, so this is left neatly cut and the top closed with a staple and finished with a bow.

Doyley Bag

Handkerchiefs require a certain amount of ingenuity to achieve a good disguise, and have been seen to be converted into flowers and put into fantasy packaging like parasols and lanterns. One of the prettiest and most simple to make is this idea which is inspired by the charming way the continental ladies make containers for rolls on the dinner table.

The shape is basically a circle. Six points are drawn at equal intervals round the perimeter and inward folds made from these points to the centre (Fig. 1). Holes are then punched on either side of the fold line and ribbon or cord threaded through and drawn up. This will form the attractive scalloped shape (Fig. 2). All kinds of paper can be used, even brown wrapping paper can be attractive when a paper doyley is placed over it and ribbon used to draw it together.

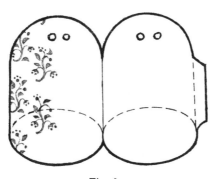

Fig. 1

Fig. 2

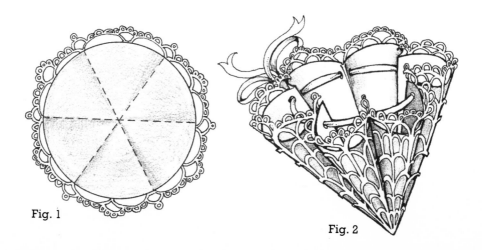

Fig. 1

Fig. 2

Boxes

Gifts of all kinds are given special protection when put in a box, and some boxes whether they are decorated, stitched or painted can be gifts in themselves. From pills and snuff, to hats and collars, or jewellery and perfume to chocolates and sewing materials, the uses of boxes are endless and this ancient container is as important today as it always has been.

Boxes can be made with stiff paper, card or papier-mâché, some beautiful examples of these are seen in the products from Kashmir, where they adorn them with the most elaborate patterns composed of masses of tiny flowers. The boxes are made of papier-mâché and hardened by a layer of varnish, as are the boxes which can be made with a long single spiral of coloured paper.

Use paper on a roll for this type of box, cut into a thin strip and wound into a flat reel. It is then ready to ease gently into the required shape. It is important not to make any change in shape too suddenly otherwise it will collapse. When the base of the box has been made the lid can be made in the same way, and the edge adjusted to fit snugly.

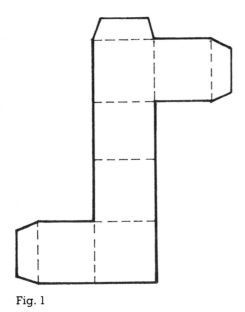

Fig. 1

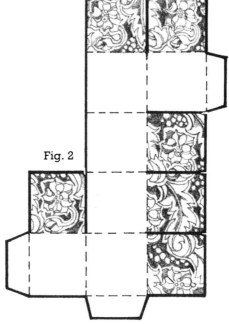

Fig. 2

The Cube Box

The conventional material for boxmaking is card, and this can be used for a variety of patterns. To make a cube mark up a row of four squares with one above the fourth square and one below the first square for the lid and the base. Add to one of the ends the flap to join the box, with extra flaps on each of the top and base squares (Fig. 1). Whenever flaps are required cut them parallel to the edges of the box. Remember that they must be inserted into the box and so should be trimmed at the corners as shown. There is only one point where glue is necessary on the simple cube box shape, and that is on the flap at the side which secures the box assembly. If the box requires strengthening, an extra square has to be added to each facet of the box (Fig. 2), and this is then folded inside.

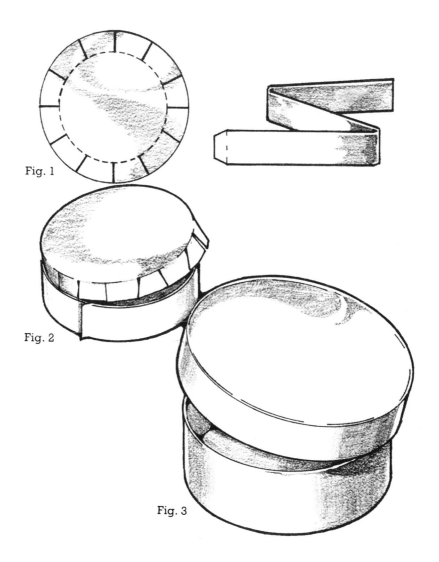

Fig. 1

Fig. 2

Fig. 3

The Pill Box

The pill box drum shape is extremely attractive, and ideal for decoration. It is made with two simple shapes, a disc and a strip. First mark a disc of the required size with a larger circle round it to form the tabs, and cut these regularly from the area between the two circles (Fig. 1). Score the smaller disc and bend the flaps up. Apply glue to each one and surround them all with the strip of card. This will require a little glue at the join (Fig. 2).

The lid is made by the same process as the base, but remember to make the original disc a fraction larger so that it will fit over the top (Fig. 3). An oval box can be made in exactly the same way and lends itself equally to various forms of decoration.

Triangular Box

Apart from the familiar shaped boxes there are many unusual ones based on various geometric shapes such as cones, triangles, hexagons, and pentagons. To make a triangular box mark out three consecutive rectangles, each with an equilateral triangle on both ends, and an extra strip along the side for the flap (Fig. 1).

Score all along the joints, apply glue to the flap and assemble the ends by folding them into place, securing the third one with glue (Fig. 2). Decoration on this is very successful when influenced by the triangular shape of the box itself. The pentagon and the hexagon shapes are made and assembled in a similar way, the facets of the boxes providing numerous areas for decoration.

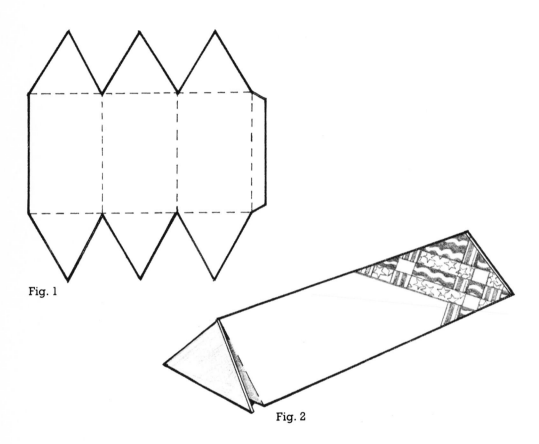

Fig. 1

Fig. 2

Pillow Pack

As an alternative there is the pillow pack, which is particularly suitable for soft fillings. This is really a flattened tube which is opened into a packet by the curved fold at each end. First mark two adjoining rectangles with curved ends and score a corresponding curve into each rectangle at both ends (Fig. 1). Add a flap to one side and apply glue to this to secure the tube when it is folded into position. Bend the ends along the curved lines until they spring into position, and an elegant pillow with emphasised corners is produced (Fig. 2).

54

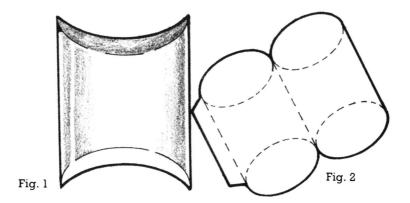

Fig. 1

Fig. 2

Decorating Boxes

Decoration is always a great delight to add, whether it is kept to the minimum or is complicated and elaborate. At the hand of the draughtsman a box is always an invitation for decorative pattern making. Geometric shapes which echo those of the box itself provide a good starting point for the beginner, or in the case of a box with corners these can provide the starting point for decoration. If not painted, the decoration can be applied using various papercrafts, simple flat areas of colour, or paper images. The shapes of the boxes themselves will suggest which to use.

Paper cut-outs are a lacy form of flat decoration which lend themselves to box decoration, or alternatively, paper doyleys are ideal for the purpose, particularly for round boxes. Strips of paper can be interwoven on the top of the box and the plain strips taken over the sides, or three different shades can be plaited together and then used for decoration.

However, paper twine is the most versatile, as the flexibility gives scope for a large range of designs, whether producing a simple outline, covering a completely solid area, or forming a

tracery of basket-type weave, the possibilities are endless.

Strips of paper can be used for quilling. This is ideal for decoration whether it provides emphasis for a flat pattern, fills an entire pattern alone, or is made to stand up in relief on the top of a box.

Paper straws lend themselves to making stars, which spring from a point on the lid. Braids and cord can be made to wind their way around or across the box.

One point to consider is the expected life of the box in relationship to the decoration and the amount of time it will take. Keepsake boxes are worthy of an extravagant use of time, and the decoration consequently can be intricate and detailed.

There are some extremely expert box designers who have naturally been inspired by little objects. The products available in the shops reflect this and themselves give inspiration to the would-be boxmaker.

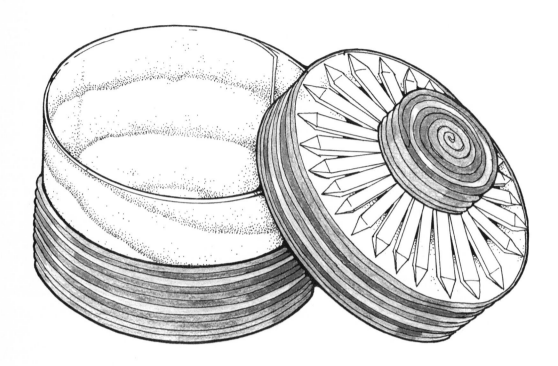

This little wooden box has been decorated entirely with paper twine.

Easter Eggs

At Eastertime the traditional shape of the boxes is changed to egg-shaped containers. Normally made of papier-mâché, these decorative caskets have enjoyed elaborate decoration since the inventive Victorians applied their natural aptitude for transforming the simplest objects to those of intricate beauty.

First make the papier-mâché eggs (see Chapter 3), and then decorate them at will with layers of thin paper, foil, additional cords, lace, sequins, and ribbons, making the surface into an intricate pattern. There are two ways of displaying eggs, either hanging, or by separating the two halves to contain a gift or chocolates inside.

There is also a growing tradition, particularly in America, of using decorated eggs of various kinds to hang from the bough of a tree. These are heavily decorated ornaments which bear little relevance to Easter other than their shape. They claim a position in American homes purely for decorative purposes. Often real eggs, they are lavishly adorned with all manner of decoration, and encrusted with tiny ornaments. The type of papercraft which can contribute to this special form of decoration is traditional quilling, or paper filigree. These eggs can be made entirely of paper filigree which, when the egg is removed, leaves a delicate, lacy, egg-shaped casket.

Crackers

Crackers

Crackers are traditionally British, being a decorative form of gift wrapping which adorns a festive table. The custom of pulling crackers is the highlight of the celebration. Two people have a tug-of-war and pull apart the cracker which bangs in the process. The person left holding the centre portion claims the small gift inside which often falls out in the general hilarity.

The custom of crackers began in the nineteenth century when Tom Smith, a sweet manufacturer, decided to put small gifts inside the wrappings of his sweets. The first crackers were actually called 'bon-bons' and the characteristic bang was not added until later. The gift was intended only as a small memento rather than as something of any real value. This is still the case today although crackers have long since lost their sweet filling.

Today's crackers are elaborate paper decorations which often contain a disappointingly trivial filling. The great advantage of making crackers at home is that the gifts can be chosen to suit the recipients.

To make successful crackers you will need an extra piece of equipment: a pair of formers. These are the hard tubes around which the paper is rolled to form the shape of the cracker. They are approximately 4·5 cm (1¾ in) in diameter and the long tube is 25 cm (10 in) in length and the shorter 13 cm (5 in). Metal or plastic formers can be bought from specialist shops and stockists but it is possible to make a perfectly adequate substitute in the home.

Use the inside of a roll of household foil or similar tube and cut into two pieces of the required length. These will not be sufficiently strong by themselves so they must be reinforced by covering in a further layer of cardboard. An old cereal packet is suitable for this. Fix the outer coating over the tube using strong adhesive tape.

Making Crackers

For one cracker you require:—
  A piece of crepe paper 30 cm
    (12 in) × 16 cm (6¼ in)
  A piece of lining paper 28 cm
    (11 in) × 15 cm (6 in)
  A piece of card 15 cm (6 in) × 9 cm
    (3½ in)
  A snap
  A motto
  A gift
  Formers
  A piece of strong string
  Glue

Tie the string to an immovable object such as the table leg and draw it over the surface towards you. Place the piece of crepe over this on the table. Then place the piece of lining paper on top following the direction of the crepe paper, but allowing plenty of crepe visible at the top for the glue area (Fig. 1). Apply a thin line of glue to the edge of the paper to secure the roll.

The motto and the snap are then placed on top of the lining paper, and, finally, the piece of card across everything. The position of the card must be correct as this supports the central area in which the gift is contained, so care should be taken at this stage to ensure that it is centrally placed (Fig. 2).

Place the pair of formers so that the join is in line with the right side of the card (Fig. 3). Keeping them both in line roll all the papers round the formers.

Then carefully ease the smaller former out slightly until the gap between the two is approximately 4·5 cm (1¾ in) (Fig. 4). Pass the string round the papers, an equal distance between the two formers and pull it as tightly as possible. This will pull the paper into a crease which chokes the end of the cracker and draws the two formers towards each other (Fig. 5). Care should be taken to guide them carefully into continuous alignment. Release the string and remove the small former, and turn the cracker round in preparation for completing the second end.

First drop the gift inside the cracker by means of the long former, which should still be inside the cracker. Gently ease this former out until it has passed the card and travelled a further 4·5 cm (1¾ in). It should be possible to feel this, and sometimes if the paper is fine enough, the difference can be detected if the cracker is held up against the light.

Before the second choking process is undertaken it is advisable to check that the gift is not trapped inside the former, but has actually passed through into the cardboard area of the cracker. Finally choke the second end in the same way as the first. It is necessary to press the former and card together slightly whilst the string is in the choking position to make a crisp edge to the tubular parts.

Most lightweight papers, such as tissue paper, wrapping paper and paper-backed foil, can be used for the main body of the cracker. The paper should be able to be torn apart easily. In the case of a strong paper, to avoid any embarrassing tustle at the table, it is advisable to run a line of holes with a tailor's wheel, or score gently along the crease line, before beginning on the cracker.

The cracker is now all ready to decorate, and the additions can be as simple or elaborate as time will allow. One point to remember, though, is that

Fig. 1

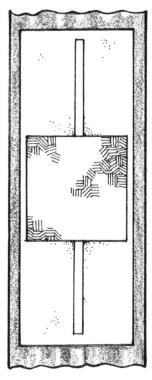

Fig. 2

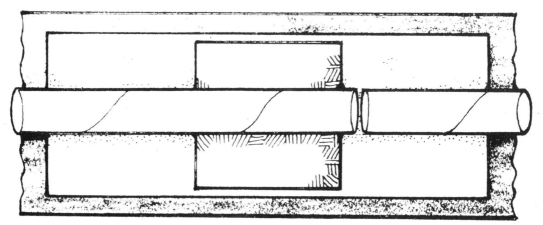

Fig. 3

Fig. 4

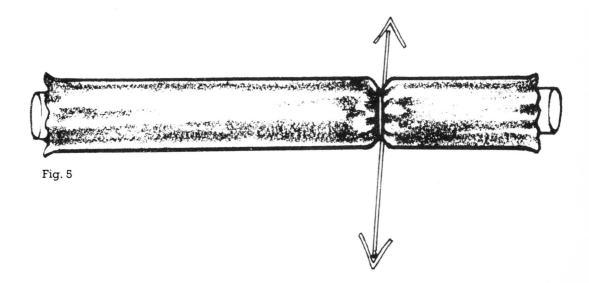

Fig. 5

crackers have always been made to be destroyed, and this should be borne in mind when choosing decoration.

There are various ways of making different designs on crackers, such as the addition of a small picture in the centre of the cracker in the form of a scrap, or other three-dimensional object, e.g. flowers, bows, cones, animals, butterflies and snowmen. It is worthwhile testing the cracker with the decoration, because if the decoration is too heavy the cracker will keep rolling over. A simple covering of some special or toning paper, or a metallic paper, makes excellent decoration for the centre area, whilst the ends also deserve some decoration.

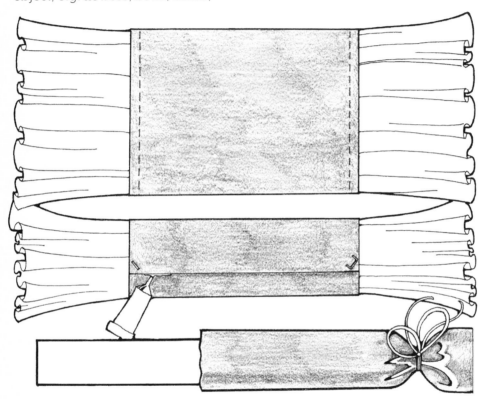

The giant cracker may need extra glue to hold the cover paper together.

A small tube is used as a former for the miniature cracker.

Giant and Miniature Crackers

As well as making regular sized crackers it is possible to make a giant cracker containing many gifts for a children's party or miniature crackers for the Christmas tree.

Use fairly stiff paper for the giant cracker; coloured cover paper is ideal for the centre of the cracker as it is firm enough to hold its own shape. The ends may be made of double crepe paper. Frill the double crepe and pleat the ends until it fits the cover paper. Sew together using a sewing machine as this will facilitate pulling the cracker.

Miniature crackers can be made from crepe paper but look very attractive when made from paper-backed foil. Any thin cylinder is suitable for use as formers: an individual cigar case would be ideal or any household tube such as surplus gas tubing.

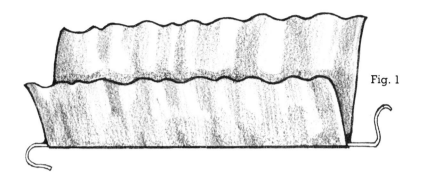

Fig. 1

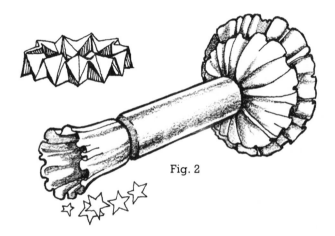

Fig. 2

Cracker Frills

Frills of varying sizes give crackers an attractive finish. Small frills can be made by merely easing out the edge of the crepe paper. Very large frills have the advantage of making the cracker appear exotic and extravagant. They are much simpler to make than they appear, and happily conceal any mishaps which may have occurred during the process of manufacturing the cracker itself.

Cut a piece of matching paper 30 cm (12 in) × 13 cm (5 in) and fold it in half lengthways, insert a piece of thin wire into the fold (Fig. 1) and gather it up as tightly as possible. Join it to the cracker by twisting the ends together round the crease. When the frills are in position, separate the layers and ease them out so that they form an arc of frills which end where the cracker is placed on the table either side (Fig. 2).

There are many variations on these frills. For example the edges may be dipped into glue and then into glitter; this is particularly advisable for papers where the edges are not well-defined, as the glitter makes the outline stronger. On some stiffer papers a simple cut out edge like zig-zag or scallops is effective. An extremely decorative edge can be achieved on crepe paper by rolling the edges. This is not easy to do, but stretching out the creases in the crepe paper results in a large undulating frill.

Ideas for Decorating Crackers

When you have mastered the basic art of making crackers it is possible to experiment with an infinite variety of decorative techniques.

Fig. 1 shows a cracker with the ends slightly frilled and decorated with zig-zag shapes cut from toning paper and attached after making the basic cracker.

Fig. 2 shows a cracker made from paper-backed foil decorated with little bells. These are made from circles of two-coloured acetate foil folded and stapled into bell shapes and then attached to the cracker.

Fig. 3 shows a motif cut from paper-backed foil which is glued into position allowing the points to curl free. The creases are decorated with decorative bows in silver twine. Tinsel makes a pretty alternative to twine and can be tied round the crease in a similar way.

Fig. 4 shows a cracker made from foil crepe. The ends of the cracker are folded and frilled in the manner of the Double Bells (see page 132) and the whole is decorated with a motif cut from a silver doyley.

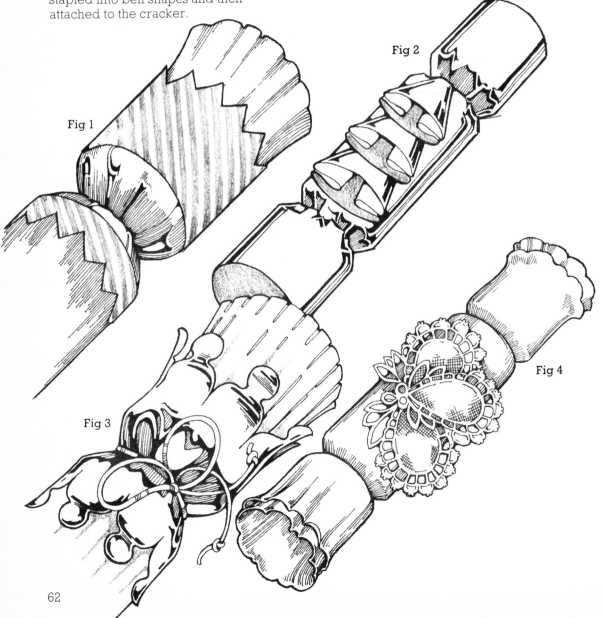

Fig 1

Fig 2

Fig 3

Fig 4

Pictures

The word picture conjures up a panel displayed on a wall whose function is solely to give pleasure to the viewer. The contents of the frame of a picture can be representational or entirely abstract. Both forms have been an essential element in interior design for centuries. The world of fine art is one to be admired and enjoyed, the abundance of talent is such that there is an endless supply of material from which the amateur can gain inspiration.

The craft of paper collage is a fascinating form of picture-making where the background plays an essential part in the design, and also provides a decorative surface on which to work. Paper can be secured to the surface at vital points, increasing the scope for design. This is particularly important in the type of collage in which layers of paper are built up and attached flat or shaped to produce interesting textures and relief work. All the basic methods of handling the paper, rolling, curling, gathering, pleating, twisting and, of course, cutting, can be used in the art of paper collage.

One of the oldest forms of the craft was created by Victorian ladies, who would while away their leisure hours rolling tiny strips of paper into tight curls, scrolls and other beautiful shapes to assemble for paper filigree work. This form of decoration was called quilling and was so named because the tight rolls of paper were made round the quill of a feather. With their resourceful minds they made all manner of intricate designs and made them into decorative borders, covered boxes and even whole cabinets.

Paper Twine Lady

One of the most flexible types of paper to use is paper twine. This can be simply twisted in the fingers so it is surprising to discover that it is quite possible to use a spinning wheel to produce the twine. This has, naturally, a great advantage as a time-saver where a large amount of twine is required. The twine tends to become slightly overspun in spite of constant regulation of tension, but this is of little consequence as it can easily be adjusted when the twine is attached to the design. The Pygmalion Lady is made entirely with crepe paper, and the majority is in the form of twine; with the emphasis of real crepe paper frills, the curls in her hair and the profusion of large feathers in her hat the design has a three-dimensional quality.

To make the Lady you will need:—

Green crepe paper, one strip cut across the grain 2·5 cm (1 in) wide

Brown crepe paper, one strip cut across the grain 2·5 cm (1 in) wide

Orange crepe paper, eight strips cut across the grain 2·5 cm (1 in) wide

White crepe paper, two strips cut across the grain 2·5 cm (1 in) wide

Cartridge paper for the outline template

Glue

First draw the outline of the Pygmalion Lady on the piece of cartridge paper, holding her parasol and her handbag.

Spin or twist all the crepe paper into twine, except one of the pieces of white as this should be reserved for frills. Apply glue to an area of the surface approximately 10 cm (4 in) square, or an area which is

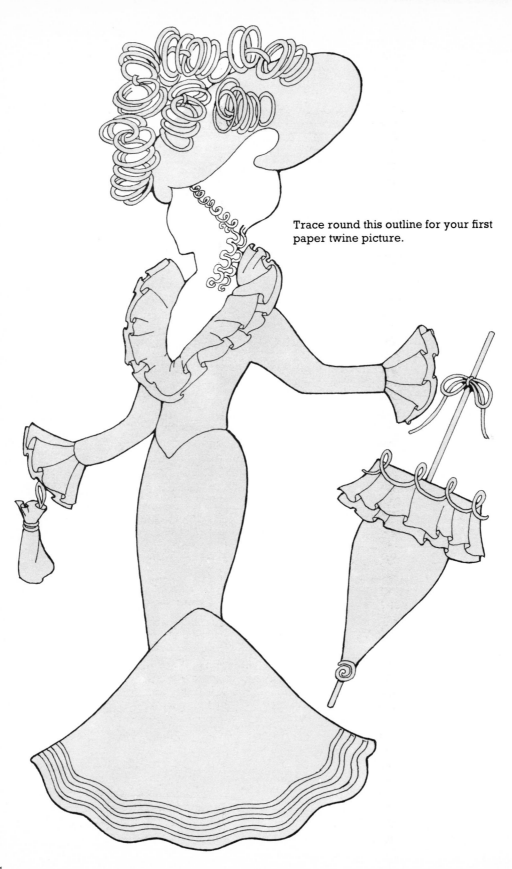

Trace round this outline for your first paper twine picture.

contained by the design, then, working from the outside into the centre, work the twine into the shape. The direction of the lines created by the twine will bear direct relation to the feeling of movement. This is similar to shading on a line drawing, so careful consideration is necessary before starting to apply the twine.

Work the fan shape on the skirt first, then take the twine upwards portion by portion. Before working the arms the tiny frills should be attached so that the twine can be used to cover the join at the wrist. The hair is worked with strips which are cut to the required length after the curls have been made by twisting a piece of twine round a needle. The feathers are produced in exactly the same way, but instead of using a needle to create the spiral the strips are wound round a pencil, then secured by tying the loops together and allowing them to spring apart.

The handbag is made by folding a tiny piece of white, frilled paper in half and tying it with a piece of orange twine. The loop is hidden inside the frills at her wrist. Most of the umbrella is made in the same way as the dress. The frill is added to the top and the spikes outlined with a piece of orange twine. Finally the handle is made by twisting a piece of brown twine until it doubles up so that the loop forms the handle, which is tied with a tiny piece of twine.

Once the Lady is completed, cut the entire shape out, allowing the areas to separate where necessary as they are easy to reassemble onto the correct backing. This may seem an unnecessary extra process when the whole design could well have been made on the correct backing in the first place. However this does protect the precious backing from possible mishaps during assembly, particularly with free-flowing glues like Uhu where tell-tale streams can ruin hours of work. The Lady, once mounted onto her gold card background, can be displayed in a pre-cut oval mount, which adds a charming finish before adding a square frame.

Giant Sunflower

The fascination of spinning crepe paper may well lead to over-production, and so a further use must be found for the twine. A complete contrast in size to the last picture, this giant sunflower incorporates not only paper twine in a simple form but also wired, crocheted and used as binding. This, together with flat coloured paper and frilled crepe paper, is cut and curled and combined to form this dramatic collage. Layer upon layer of different materials and textures are superimposed to produce this conglomerate effect.

This type of technique lends itself particularly to the simple shape of the sunflower, because this contrasts well with the complex composition. The complicated patterns created by the amassed florets have been the cause of constant intrigue to mathematicians and artists alike for centuries, and are no less inviting to us now.

To make the sunflower you will need:—
    Sheet of backing card
    1 strip each of green, brown and
        orange 2·5 cm (1 in) wide
        1 disc of gold backing card
        13 cm (5 in) diameter
    10 strips brown crepe paper cut
        across grain 2 cm (1 in) wide
    15 strips orange crepe paper cut
        across grain 2 cm (1 in) wide
    1 strip orange crepe paper cut
        across roll 13 cm (5 in) wide
    1 sheet yellow paper
    1 sheet orange paper
    1 sheet cream paper (these papers
        are lightweight drawing paper
        which is printed with one colour
        over the entire surface producing
        a matt finish)
    Green double crepe paper for the
        leaves
    Curved strip of card for the stem
    12 thin stem wires, 24 gauge
    3 covered stem wires
    Glue
    Sellotape
Spin all the orange crepe paper into

65

Imaginative decoration can transform even the simplest box into something special.

1　Large cube box of coloured card
2　Cube box covered in square printed paper
3　Cube box of foil card decorated with zig-zag scraps of paper
4　Conical box
5　Sphere wrapped as top hat
6　Cube decorated with interwoven strips of coloured tissue
7　Pill box decorated with tissue flower
8　Sphere wrapped as a flower
9　Decoration on a box emphasized by paper twine
10　Pillow pack
11　Wooden box decorated with paper twine
12　Cube box decorated with paper straws

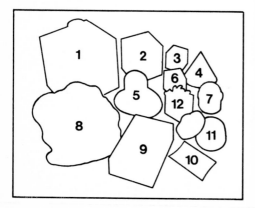

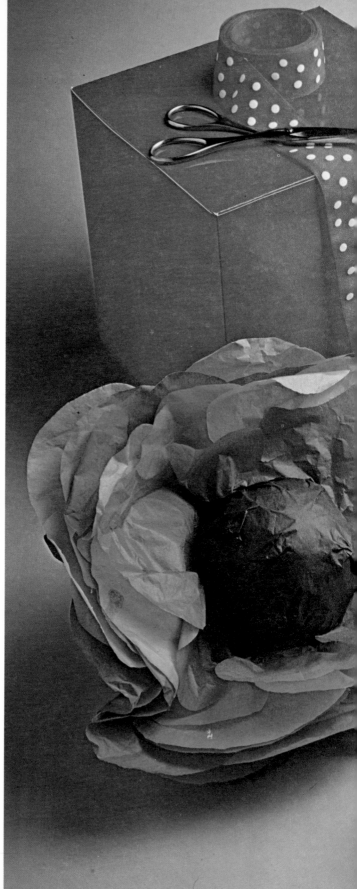

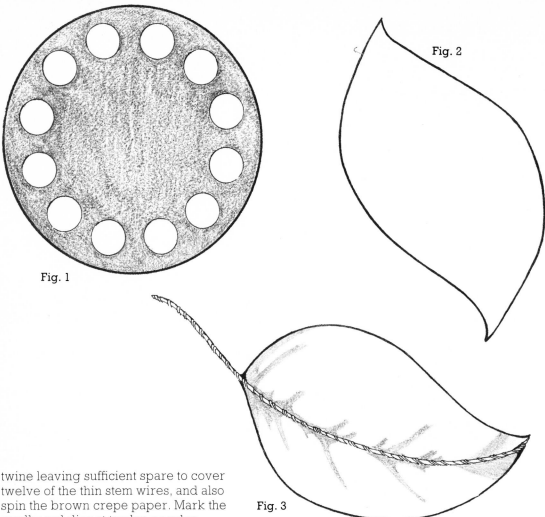

Fig. 1

Fig. 2

Fig. 3

twine leaving sufficient spare to cover twelve of the thin stem wires, and also spin the brown crepe paper. Mark the cardboard disc at twelve regular intervals around the edge (Fig. 1).

Cut twelve curved petal shapes 13 cm (5 in) long × 5 cm (2 in) wide, from the piece of yellow paper. Fold the paper in half before cutting and cut two layers at once so that the irregular shape is mirrored and can then be used with the curves undulating in alternate directions (Fig. 2).

Use the wires which are covered with the orange crepe paper and apply glue to one side of their entire length. Place one onto the centre of each of the petal shapes ensuring that the wires reach the tip of each one (Fig. 3).

When the glue is dry the petals can be shaped by gently bending the wire into a double curve to give an undulating appearance. Pinch the base of each one and thread it into a hole in

the cardboard disc, securing the position at the back with sellotape (Fig. 4).

Use the orange paper twine: finger crochet the whole length and then shape it into a zig-zag (Figs. 5 and 6). Fix every alternate point to the disc at the point at which the petal is inserted. The other points of the zig-zag will then stand free above the surface of the petals.

Next, unravel the brown, green and orange strips and, holding them all together roll them loosely into one large roll. Secure the roll with a little glue. Working all along one of these surfaces ease the crepe paper into a frilled spiral and then press it flat so that all three colours are clearly

68

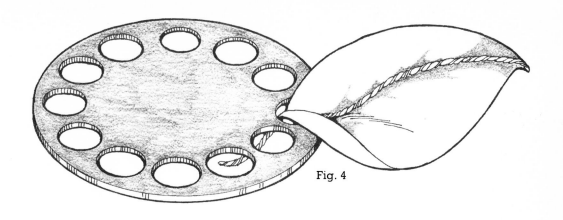

Fig. 4

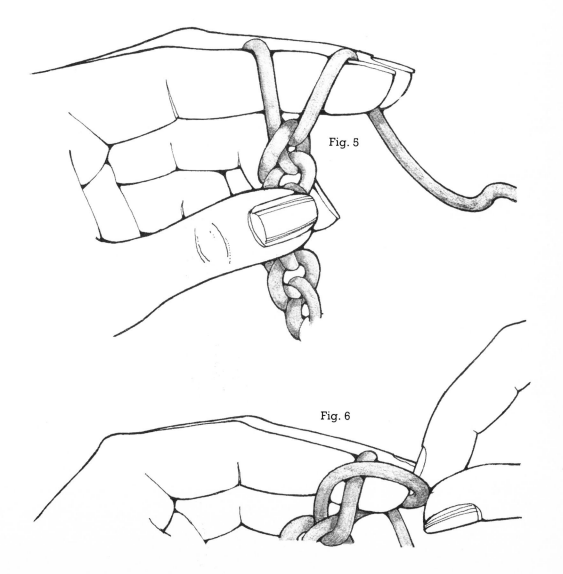

Fig. 5

Fig. 6

69

Gold, silver and white are the dominant colours used for this collection of festive crackers.

1 White crepe cracker decorated with gold paper and concertina rings of acetate foil
2 Gold and silver foil used both for the cracker and the decoration
3 Grey crepe cracker frilled at the ends and set off with a simple design in silver twine
4 Paper-backed gold foil cracker decorated with the edge of a silver doyley
5 Foil crepe cracker decorated with a motif cut from a silver doyley
6 A white crepe cracker with petal-like frills is set off by gold decoration
7 Gold crepe paper with a simple design makes a sophisticated cracker

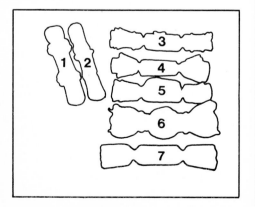

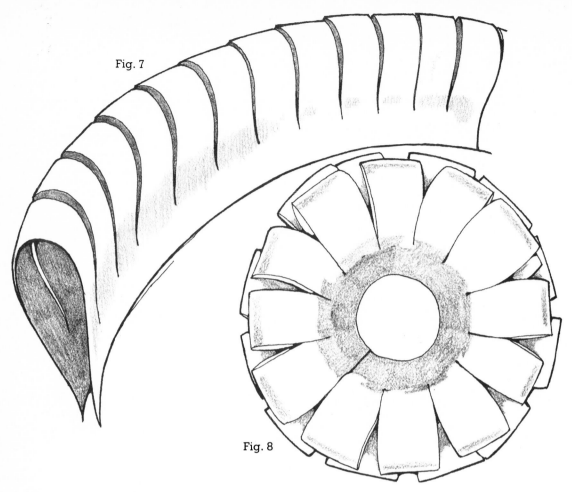

Fig. 7

Fig. 8

visible. Attach this to the centre of the disc so that there is ample space for the two rows of little florets to stand all round.

Each floret is made with orange or cream coloured paper and there are twelve of each colour. To make one cut a piece of the paper 6 cm (2¼ in) × 4 cm (1½ in), fold it in half lengthways and make parallel cuts three-quarters of the way into the strip so that it resembles a comb (Fig. 7). Curl each cut piece outwards and roll it round the pencil. Secure with glue before removing it, then apply a ring of glue to the base and place it in position (Fig. 8).

This completes the flower, all except for the frill of orange crepe which gives a sunny surround and makes the flower head stand off the surface. This is made by simply stitching the wide orange strip onto a piece of wire and

gathering it until it fits nicely round the flower, with the petals just reaching the perimeter (Fig. 9). First attach the frill to the backing surface with a liberal quantity of glue and leave it to dry securely before adding the petal structure in the same way.

To support the flowerhead the stem is made by binding the brown paper twine round the stem shape (Fig. 10) and gluing it into position.

The leaves complete the picture and are very simple to make. Put a piece of covered stem wire, which has been shaped into a leaf, onto a piece of double crepe and secure with glue. When it is dry the superfluous paper can be cut away and the spare wire twisted together to form the stem of the leaf (Fig. 11). This should be tucked under the edge of the main stem and a little extra glue added to the tip of the leaf when it is in position.

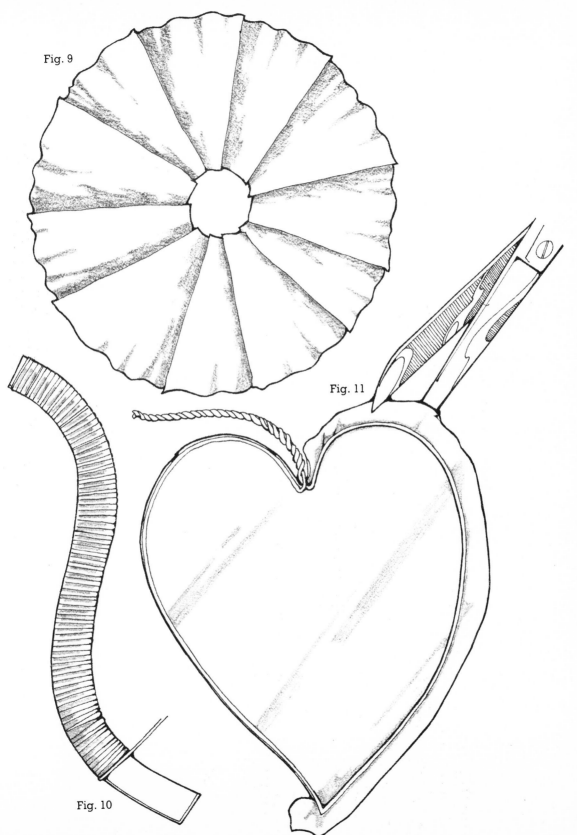

Fig. 9

Fig. 10

Fig. 11

Left Giant Sunflower
Above right Paper Twine Lady
Below right Paper Twine Garland and
Miniature Sunflower

The variation in size and mood of these
pictures emphasizes the versatility of
paper as a medium for wall decoration.

Miniature Sunflower

The fascinating sunflower can also be adapted to make a bright miniature picture.

You will need:—
    Strip of white paper 0·5 cm ($\frac{1}{4}$ in) wide
    Thin red paper 30 cm (12 in) × 2·5 cm (1 in)
    Thin yellow paper 30 cm (12 in) × 2·5 cm (1 in)
    Backing card
    Round frame 10 cm (4 in) diameter
    Glue

Use the pale yellow thin paper for the petals and cut several tiny pointed oval shapes 2·5 cm (1 in) long. The number of these will vary according to the way in which they are packed round the picture, there are approximately 40 here. Curl the tip of each petal and attach it to the surface with glue so that the frame pushes the curl away from the backing. Then place a second row inside the first and a third row inside that.

The thin red paper is used for the stamens; cut six pieces of equal length from the strip. Make a row of tiny parallel cuts into the strips along the long sides until they resemble combs. Curl all the cut ends, place the pieces so that they curl downwards and attach the uncut parts with glue, following the circular pattern of the petals. These pieces should fill the centre.

The contrast in texture of the concentric rings gives this simple picture added interest.

Use the strip of white paper to roll seven tight quilled rolls and glue them into the centre in a cluster which covers the join of red paper.

Paper Twine Garland

This charming miniature picture is made entirely from single crepe paper, with no other form of support than the glue which holds the design against the background. Paper twine is ideal for such minute work, not only for its scale but also because of its flexibility. The little flowers are made by tying a knot with four twists in it, simply pulling it tight and cutting the ends as close to the knot as possible.

The stem which forms the ring around which the flowers and bows nestle, is a single piece of twine with some little leaves. These are formed by making a single knot before joining to a loop. These leaves are joined to the stem by using an additional strip of crepe paper and binding the stem a second time, adding the leaves at regular intervals.

Arrange the ring so that it echoes the shape of the frame and then apply the glue to the back and fix it in position. The paper twine bows are arranged at intervals, interspersed with the little flowers.

For this type of three-dimensional design a domed glass is preferable. If only a flat one is available however, it may be possible to pack the area between the glass and the backing with paper twine. This could form part of the design blending with the colour scheme within the frame, as it will, of course, be visible. This frame is only 7·5 cm (3 in) in diameter, so the flowers are indeed minute. It would be a welcome gift for someone who has a small house with limited space for decorative objects.

77

These hats and masks show how much fun can be had from dressing up without the trouble of making complete costumes.

1 Edwardian hat
2 Clown hat and ruff
3 Bonnet
4 Paper bag mask
5 Pumpkin mask
6 Carnival mask
7 Beads

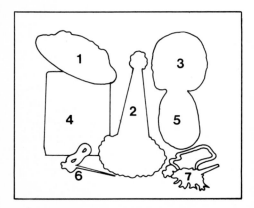

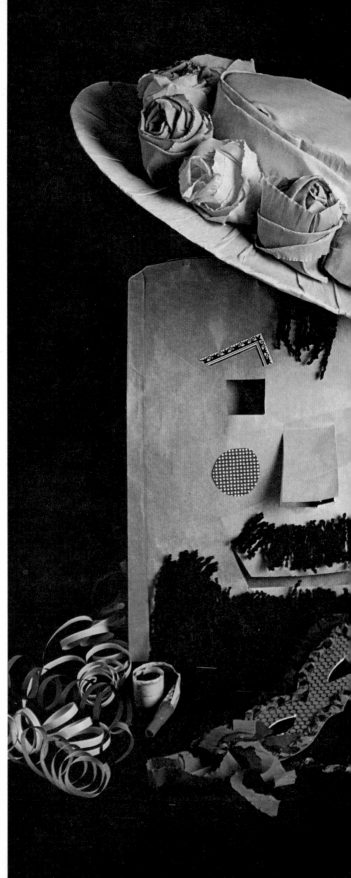

Paper Sculpture

The essence of paper sculpture is clarity of line with the crisp edges emphasised only by shadows cast by overlapping layers. All the different shapes are produced by combinations of folding or curving. The moulding is regulated by straight pleats or curved folds.

Accuracy is absolutely essential for the neat effect required for paper sculpture, and so wherever possible it is advisable to use a ruler, compass and any other precision instrument you find helpful. Regular folds will, of course, require measuring. Where a sharp edge is required at the apex or point of a curve or fold, the line should first be scored on the outside of the fold.

The type of design suitable for this sort of work should always be very simple. Stylized images with exaggerated characteristics are often effective. The sort of characteristics which can be successfully exaggerated are feathers on large birds, scales, dramatic hair styles or large hats. In this case the beautiful fan tail of the dove has been chosen as a focal point.

The illustration shows just one example of this type of work. It is essentially very simple being made entirely from pleated, rolled and curved paper. You will find after a little experimentation that you will quickly be able to invent your own designs.

Costumes

There is something very special about the transitory quality of a balloon, a bunch of flowers, and a paper costume, and lavish attention to their manufacture is far from wasted. Often a special occasion, festival, fancy dress party or concert can demand the sort of costume which can economically be made from paper. A lavish use of paper will not only provide strength, but also an appearance of reality. Paper allows exotic costumes to be made far beyond the scope of conventional material in the kaleidoscope of colours, and exaggerated emphasis on details like hats, frills and trimmings.

Paper can often pass as the real thing, especially in theatre work. For example, real small feathers may not be sufficiently stylized to be seen from a distance, whereas layers of shaped crepe paper would create the desired effect.

Paper, which is, of course, naturally fragile is particularly vulnerable to the wear and tear of being used as adornment, so the use of strong material is essential. Crepe paper is the best to use for soft clothes as the flexibility allows for greater movement before the paper reaches tearing point. However, this is not always strong enough to support the dramatic shapes which some of the costumes require. Thick cover paper is ideal for this, and can be used alone or covered with suitable decorative papers. The nature of the materials means that costumes made with paper have to be somewhat stylized, but this is often an advantage. The situations which demand the use of paper are often special occasions when the clothes will be used only once. By moulding the papers and stitching the crepe some interesting effects can be achieved.

Masks

Carnival Mask

A fancy dress party often requires little more than a mask, or perhaps a head-dress, and the carnival mask is an enchanting one to wear.

For the mask you will need:—
   Three colours of crepe paper cut into strips 2·5 cm (1 in) wide
   1 strip of crepe 10 cm (4 in) wide
   1 stick 30 cm (12 in) long
   A piece of sequin waste to cover the surface of the mask
   Glue
   Stapler

First cut the piece of shiny coloured card in half and place the pieces together back to back. Then cut out the mask shape (Fig. 1). Carefully measure the position of the eye holes, remembering that the wearer will want to see where to go. Frill the sides of the wide strip of crepe, and fold it in half lengthways. Apply a line of glue all round the back of one of the mask pieces and place the frills so that 2·5 cm (1 in) is visible all round on the right side (Fig. 2). Then add the second mask piece to the back so that the frill is sandwiched between the two. Decorate the front by placing the sequin waste so that it covers the surface. Only use glue at the edges where it will be covered, because the strength of the glue can have a distorting effect.

Plait the three thin strips together, leaving at least 60 cm (24 in) to

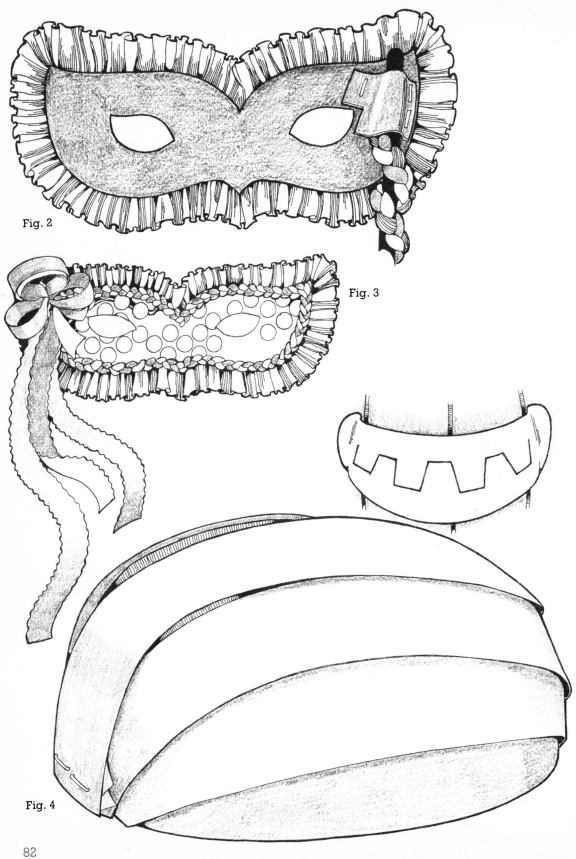

Fig. 2

Fig. 3

Fig. 4

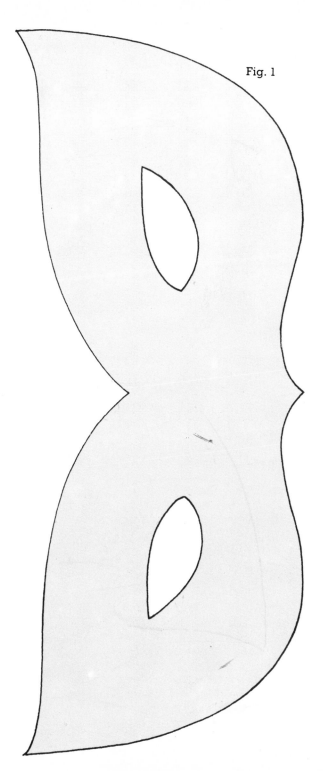

Fig. 1

decorate the handle. Glue the plait all round the mask covering the edges of the sequin waste (Fig. 3). Use one of the unplaited strips to cover the handle by rotating it so that the paper forms a spiral, then a second one the opposite way, but spaced so that both colours are visible.

Attach the handle to the back of one corner of the mask with the addition of a spare piece of shiny card. Apply some glue all round the top of the stick and then staple the card firmly to the back of the mask. It should be possible to staple the mask at points which are covered by the decoration. Then, finally, use the last remaining strip to make a bow for the corner where the mask is supported.

Hallowe'en Mask

Means of visibility is an essential element in a mask but it need not be obvious as this pumpkin Hallowe'en mask shows. It is made of strips of brown cover paper 8 cm (3 in) × 50 cm (20 in). These are joined into a dome of radiating strips and secured with staples (Fig. 4).

The facial features are made by cutting a row of smiling teeth and two eye discs from a piece of cream coloured paper. When complete the mask can be simply attached to the head with hair clips.

Carrier Bag Mask

For economy and speed it is impossible to beat the efficiency of a paper carrier bag mask. NEVER USE A POLYTHENE BAG to make a mask. If a suitable paper bag is not available it is quite easy to make one from ordinary brown wrapping paper (see page 49).

Simply mark and cut out shapes for the eyes, mouth and nose. These can be painted or decorated as required.

Beads

These beads are always great fun to make and are simple enough for the

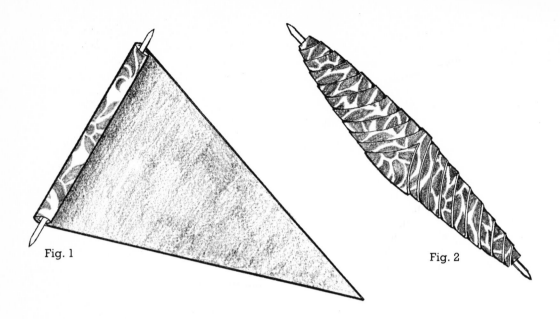

Fig. 1   Fig. 2

younger members of the family to make for themselves. They can be made up in many combinations of colours and in varying lengths into necklaces, bracelets and even ear-rings.

To make them you will need:—
   Shiny art paper in various colours
   A cocktail stick
   Glue
   Strong thread
Cut long thin triangles from the paper 2 cm ($\frac{3}{4}$ in) × 9·5 cm ($3\frac{3}{4}$ in) and 3·5 cm ($1\frac{1}{4}$ in) × 23 cm (9 in). The number of these will vary according to the project in mind.
   Each bead is made by rolling one of the triangles tightly over the cocktail stick starting with the wide end (Fig. 1). Roll so that the coloured side is outside and the spiralled edge creates a pattern on the bead (Fig. 2).
   Secure the tip with glue and allow to dry before carefully removing the cocktail stick. Using strong thread and a needle combine into strings of the desired length.

Hats

Hats can be intricate and complicated, or extremely simple, and if simplicity is required then the cone with its

various adaptations is the most suitable. For witches and wizards black paper ones are ideal, and for a clown white cartridge paper is the best to choose. With the addition of one or two decorations, or a brim, these hats can be surprisingly effective.

Clown Hat

For the clown you will need:—
   1 sheet of heavy cartridge paper
   1 roll of double crepe paper
   2 strips of different coloured crepe paper 10 cm (4 in) wide
   Paint
   Staples
   Glue
   Thin wire, 26 gauge
Cut a fan shape from the cartridge paper 40 cm (16 in) radius, use a compass, or if this does not have a large enough span it is possible to work with a thread tied to a pencil and pinned at the centre. Coil and glue into position by overlapping the straight edges. At this stage measure for a good fit (Fig. 1).
   Make four pompons by gathering a strip of crepe paper up to one spot and looping the wire thread over the

centre of the roll. Twist the ends together very tightly to make the paper spring open and coax it into the pompon shape (Fig. 2).

Push the wires through the paper hat and bend them down flat. Retain a piece of one of the crepe paper strips, fold it in half lengthways, and glue it over the edge of the hat. Use the double crepe paper for the frill and paint along one of the long edges with one colour, then turn the paper over and repeat the process on the other side. Frill the painted edges then fold the paper in half lengthways, so that both the painted edges face upwards (Fig. 3). Gather the fold onto a piece of wire and twist the ends together.

Edwardian Hat

Sometimes an occasion demands large flamboyant hats, and this is where extravagant use of crepe paper is essential. Although this flamboyant Edwardian hat uses a large amount of paper, it does not take long to make.

You will need:—
    2 sheets of cover paper
    1 roll of crepe paper for the hat
    2 rolls of crepe paper in toning colours for decorating
    Stem wires (10-12 depending on size of hat)
    Glue

First cut a circle 25 cm (10 in) radius from the cover paper for the brim of the hat, and make cuts radiating from the centre in sufficient length until the brim snugly fits the wearer (Fig. 1). These cuts should be made with caution, as once the hat has been made too big, it is impossible to make it smaller again. Place the brim on top of the second piece of cover paper, and mark round the space cut in the centre. Cut this out allowing 2·5 cm (1 in) all round for the turning. Score the original line and make cuts from the edge to the line at regular 2·5 cm (1 in) intervals all round (Fig. 2).

For the sides of the crown, cut a strip 12·5 cm (5 in) wide from the cover paper, and of sufficient length for it to overlap by 5 cm (2 in) when in position on the brim. Apply glue to all the flaps on crown and brim and assemble using the side strip to cover the flaps and hold it all together (Fig. 3).

To cover the hat cut two pieces, one for the brim and the other for the crown. The size of these will be determined by the hat itself. For the brim, cut a strip of crepe paper from the main colour whose length is slightly greater than the circumference of the brim. Before cutting, fold the paper in half lengthways so that it is double thickness and measure it, cutting 5 cm (2 in) wider than the brim. This is to ensure that it is sufficient to cover the underside of the brim as well as the top. Apply glue to both edges and

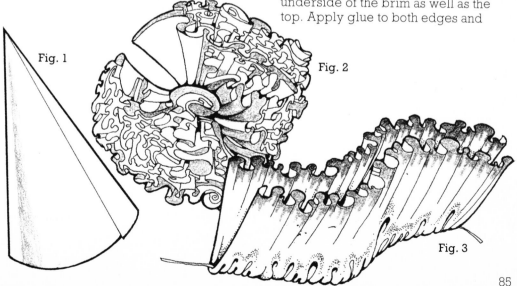

Fig. 1

Fig. 2

Fig. 3

feed the paper carefully over the brim. Make sure the paper covers the join between crown and brim inside and outside the hat. Gather the loose edges before finally fixing into place so that folds appear to radiate from the centre (Fig. 4).

Place the second piece over the crown and cut it so that it half covers the sides (Fig. 5). Cover the sides and crown with glue and attach the covering paper. Cut a strip from one piece of decorating paper 30 cm (12 in) wide, and fold over lengthways on both sides. Apply glue to the sides and fix the folded strip to this, covering up

the joins of the other crepe papers. Make a large loose bow with the remaining folded strip and attach it to one side of the hat (Fig. 6).

The cabbage roses are simply made with long 10 cm (4 in) strips of crepe paper. Attach the end to a stem wire by twisting the wire over the paper (Fig. 7). Then roll the paper over pulling it gently to form the rose shape, and finish by tucking the end into the layers underneath (Fig. 8). Make several of these roses using both colours, and twist the stems together into a long line until they fill the entire brim.

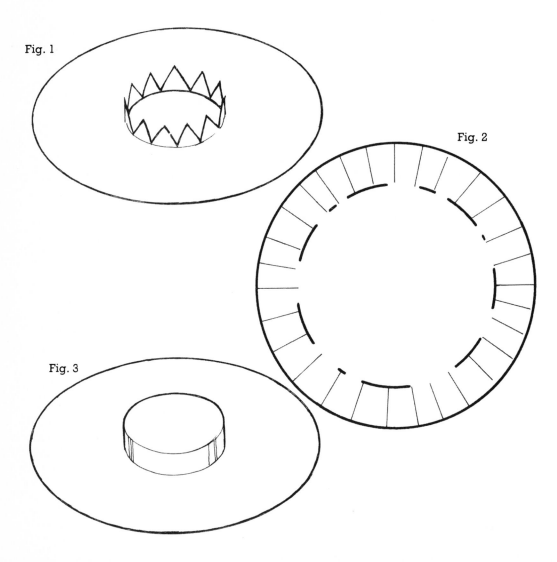

Fig. 1

Fig. 2

Fig. 3

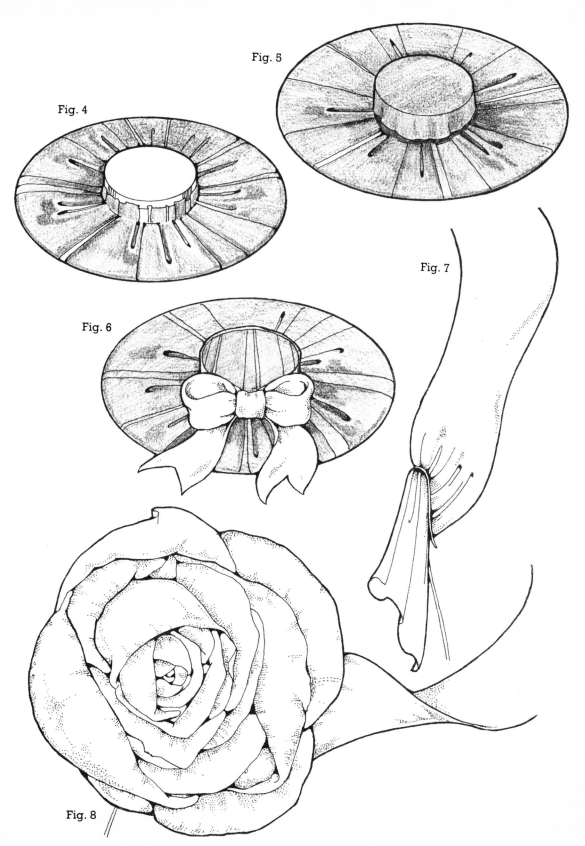

Fig. 4

Fig. 5

Fig. 6

Fig. 7

Fig. 8

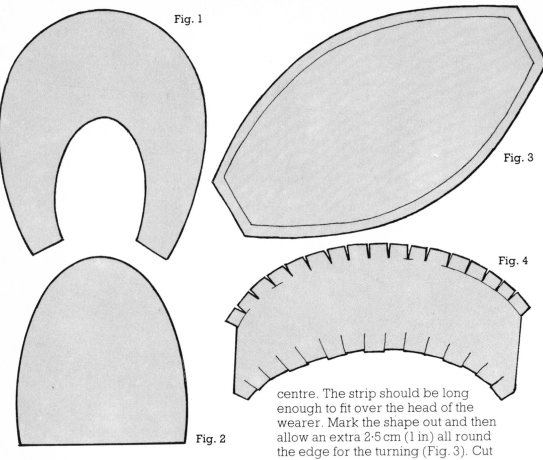

Fig. 1

Fig. 3

Fig. 4

Fig. 2

Bonnet

One other type of hat which is always flattering is the bonnet.

You will need:—
  1 sheet of coloured cover paper
  2 rolls of crepe paper for the decorations and covering
  Glue
  Binding wire

First cut the shape of the peak from the cover paper so that it fits the wearer's face snugly and stands at least 15 cm (6 in) above her face and tapers to 7·5 cm (3 in) at the lowest point each side (Fig. 1). Then, using the space that is allowed for the face as a guide, cut a small arched piece for the back (Fig. 2).

The whole bonnet is held together with a tapering strip of cover paper, whose width increases from 5 cm (2 in) at the edges to 12·5 cm (5 in) in the

centre. The strip should be long enough to fit over the head of the wearer. Mark the shape out and then allow an extra 2·5 cm (1 in) all round the edge for the turning (Fig. 3). Cut along the outside, score the inner line and make little cuts from the edge to the scored line. Bend all the flaps on one side upwards, and on the other side downwards (Fig. 4). Apply glue to all the flaps, on the outside of the band. Attach the back to the row of glue flaps and then the peak to the other (Fig. 5).

Now cut a strip from each of the colours of the crepe paper 2·5 cm (1 in) wide, and frill all along the long side of both strips. Apply glue to the entire front surface of the peak and attach the frills, using alternate colours in decreasing rows until the surface is covered (Fig. 6). There may be a little space left in the very centre of the front, but this can always be filled with a bow made with a strip of the same colour.

Next cover the back of the peak by cutting a piece of crepe paper the width of the widest part of the peak

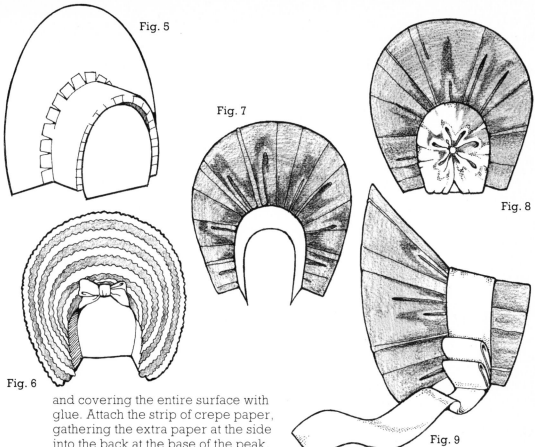

Fig. 5

Fig. 7

Fig. 8

Fig. 6

Fig. 9

and covering the entire surface with glue. Attach the strip of crepe paper, gathering the extra paper at the side into the back at the base of the peak. The loose edges here will be covered later by the sash (Fig. 7).

The back and sides of the bonnet are covered with one piece of crepe paper. This is made of a strip which is cut to the width of the side and the diameter of the back. Fold one of the long sides over 2·5 cm (1 in) to form a hem, insert a wire into the fold, and glue the hem. When it has dried gather the paper on the wire until the paper is all in one position and twist the ends of the wire together. Apply glue to the entire surface of the remaining uncovered hat, and attach the prepared crepe paper so that the gathered twist is placed centrally on the back. Ease the sides into position so that the area is completely covered (Fig. 8).

Finally complete the bonnet by making a big sash with a strip of crepe paper which is 30 cm (12 in) wide. Fold it twice into three equal parts and place it in position over the sides.

Ruche it up at the base on either side so that it can be firmly attached before it is tied together (Fig. 9).

Sometimes for fancy dress parties for children, cavalcades and carnivals a more complete costume is required than merely a head-dress. Stylized versions of stage and theatrical costumes are the best to choose, as this type of design lends itself to interpretation through paper. Over strong paper frames, frills and sometimes wire hoops, the more delicate and flimsy papers can be used. Where a simple dress is required single crepe paper is perfectly adequate, though if it is required for an energetic occasion it may be preferable to use the material double. Many of the nursery rhymes have charming characters to imitate, and out of the enormous number Little Miss Muffet has been chosen for the example.

Little Miss Muffet Costume

A pretty mob cap and dress with the traditional high waistline is flattered by the frills along the hem. Nursery rhymes so often seem to contain some macabre suggestions, in this case the poor little girl being frightened by a spider. However, the costume would not be complete without the spider so black crepe paper has been used for the accomplice.

To make Little Miss Muffet for an 8-year-old child you will need:—
    1 roll of double crepe paper
    3 rolls of single crepe paper
    1 roll of contrasting crepe paper
Use one complete roll of the single crepe for the skirt. Using a sewing machine gather one of the long edges to fit the wearer. Cut four strips of the same coloured paper to use for the frills 15 cm (6 in) wide and two of the same size in the contrasting colour. Place three of the strips together with the contrasting colour between the others and gather all the layers at once onto the lowest edge of the hem.

For the bodice and sleeves use an appropriate dress pattern with back fastenings, but remember that owing to the fragility of the material extra space should be allowed for movement. Using the double crepe, make up according to instructions.

Gather the sleeves, attach a band made of a strip of paper 5 cm (2 in) wide and fold it over to conceal the raw edge, gluing it into position (Fig. 1). Finish off the neck with a similar band. For just one occasion the costume can be simply pinned together at the back with safety pins. If hooks and eyes are required the easiest ones to attach to paper are those which can be obtained on a strip of paper, as they can be attached by machine.

Measure the waist size and cut a piece of double crepe paper 12·5 cm (5 in) wide, so that the crinkles run across the strip. Then cut a piece of the contrasting colour single crepe the

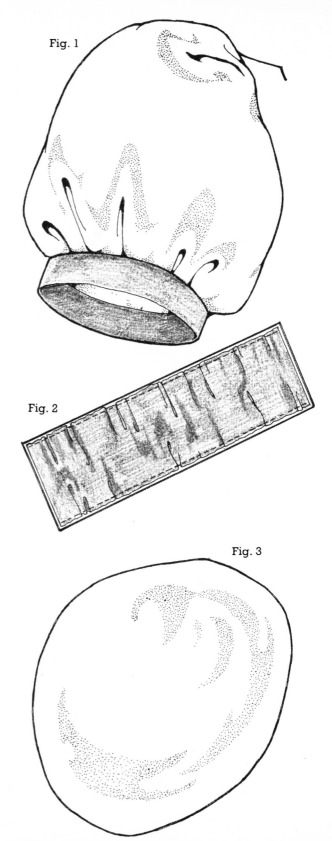

Fig. 1

Fig. 2

Fig. 3

Fig. 4

Fig. 5

same width, and stitch it to the double crepe paper, gathering it in the process. This should be done on both sides to form the wide sash (Fig. 2). Use this as the high waistband and attach the bodice and skirt to it.

The hat is made by cutting a piece of the single crepe paper 56 cm (22 in) square, rounding the corners and stretching out the centre of the paper (Fig. 3). Stitch all round the hat 10 cm (4 in) from the edge. Gather this to form the frill.

Cut a strip of the contrasting crepe paper 5 cm (2 in) wide so that it fits the head of the wearer and stitch it to the hat to form a contrasting band (Fig. 4). As a certain amount of gathering is required try to keep it regular, this will produce a shape which appears uncomfortably tall but this results in the right shape when it is pushed down on the head (Fig. 5).

The creepy spider is made with eight pieces of wire, which is simply covered with twisted black crepe paper which (cut out from strips 5 cm (2 in) wide) and then assembled by twisting the covered legs together in the centre to form the body.

91

Hawaiian Costume

Another costume which lends itself to papercraft is the Hawaiian dress which is effective but very easy to make, using only strips of brightly coloured crepe. The brightest colours should be chosen, as in a natural sunny climate only these withstand the strong rays of the sun.

To make the Hawaiian costume you will need:—
  1 roll each of orange, pink and yellow crepe paper for the garlands
  1 roll of yellow crepe paper for the grass skirt
  Stem wires

The skirt is made by cutting masses of crepe paper strips 2·5 cm (1 in) wide with the crinkles running lengthways and pulling the wrinkles out of each one until they start to shape into tubular forms. Use two of the strips together to form the waistband and stitch the strips to it (Fig. 1).

Remember to pack the strips together very tightly as they are to form a skirt which is not supposed to be transparent. For extra strength it is advisable to make one or two additional rows of stitching to withstand energetic use.

The garlands are all made with the same type of stylized flowers. The largest flowers which are used around the neck are made from strips 10 cm (4 in) wide. The medium sized flowers round the hips are 8 cm (3 in) strips. The smallest, for the head-dress and anklet, are made from strips 5 cm (2 in) wide.

To make one flower simply undo the rolled up strip of crepe paper and gather it together again, rolling it into a flower shape. Then twist a piece of stem wire tightly around the bunched paper (Fig. 2). Open the frills so that the layers form the petals.

This shape is particularly suitable and adaptable as it has already been used for the pompons on the clown hats. Attach the garland of flowers to

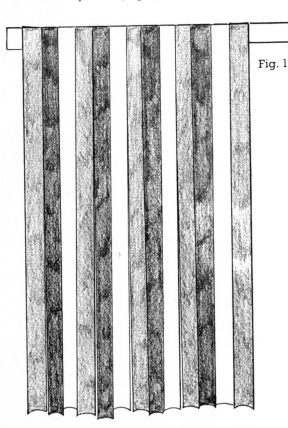

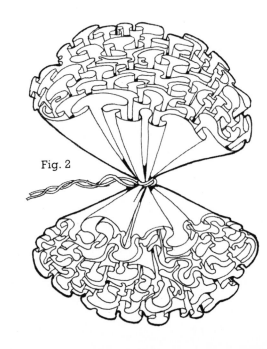

Fig. 1

Fig. 2

Fig. 1

the grass skirt by entwining the wire stems between the grasses. The skirt itself can be made any length as long as the waistband is longer than the wearer's waist measurement. It is in the shape of a long strip which can be joined at any point to the wearer's hips, wrap-over style.

Making Your Own Variations

From these two suggestions it is easy to see how dress patterns for conventional fabrics can be adapted and used for papercraft. Loose fitting and flowing shapes are the simplest, both to make and to wear. Cloaks and pointed hats are the easiest of all, and make an effective covering with relatively little work. So the less ambitious can make some stunning creations from this simple formula.

Witches, with their sinister swirling cloaks and pointed hats, require only a

black brim and a broomstick to be instantly recognisable. Another supernatural figure is the magician, whose cloak and hat can be lavishly decorated with shapes and sparkles, requiring only a magic wand and green face to complete the image.

Highwayman

A slightly sophisticated version of the cloak and dagger costume, which will certainly appeal to the young gentleman of the party, is the Highwayman's outfit. The high-collared cloak and three-cornered hat are effective by themselves, but with the addition of a black mask and a gun one can imagine the influence such a character would have on a fancy dress party.

To make the Highwayman's outfit you will need:—
    1 sheet of black cover paper
    4 rolls of black crepe paper
Use one roll of crepe paper double and attach a second roll, also double, by stitching all four layers together along one of the longest sides. This is to make the main cloak. The length can be adapted to fit the wearer.

Add the third roll of crepe paper, doubled, to the top of the long cloak by stitching along the longest side to form the smaller cape. Then measure the length of the space between the neck and shoulder and make darts so that the shoulders fit snugly (Fig. 1).

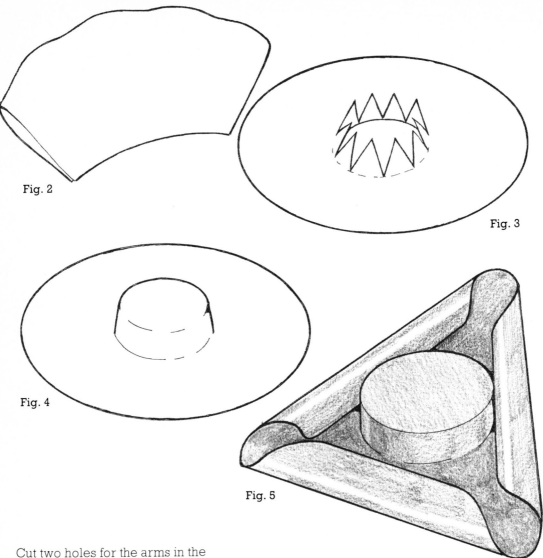

Fig. 2

Fig. 3

Fig. 4

Fig. 5

Cut two holes for the arms in the underneath layer of the cloak. Cut the collar from the last roll of crepe paper 40 cm (16 in) × 60 cm (24 in), fold it in half lengthways across the crinkles and stretch out the fold so that the collar is fan-shaped (Fig. 2). Attach it by stitching it to the inside of the neck of the cloak.

Make the hat by cutting a large round brim 25 cm (10 in) diameter from the cover paper. Cut a hole in the centre with star shaped cuts radiating from the centre until the brim fits snugly to the head. Then bend the pieces upwards and coat with glue (Fig. 3).

For the Crown cut a piece of black crepe paper 45 cm (18 in) square and then stretch the centre out to form the domed shape. Trim away the corners so that it can be placed over the brim and attached to the glued points. If the crepe paper is too stretchy a second band can be added as shown to retain the shape (Fig. 4).

Curl the brim upwards at three equidistant points by rolling them over a pencil and then joining the curls to the side of the crown with a stapler (Fig. 5).

Complete the costume by making a black mask with the cover paper.

The Parrot

There are many occasions which require an animal or bird costume and at the time these often seem daunting as they require a degree of planning, but once the basic shape has been worked and cut from cover paper, the addition of layers and layers of feather shapes can make a most effective transformation. The parrot is a handsome, brightly coloured bird to imitate and coloured crepe paper is ideal for this.

You will need:—
  3 sheets of green cover paper
  1 roll each of red, yellow, turquoise blue, royal blue and white crepe paper
  Paint
  Glue
  Staples

First cut the breastplate according to the pattern, but measure the length on the wearer who should be able to sit down in the costume, the width will also be regulated by the size of the wearer (Fig. 1).

Then cut a piece for the back, tail and shoulders, which should entirely cover the back of the wearer (Fig. 2). Join this to the breastplate with a stapler at one of the shoulders (Fig. 3).

Add an extra piece to cross under the breastplate, attaching this to the second side of the back at the shoulder (Fig. 4). This will form an opening for the neck which can be pinned together when the costume is in use.

Starting at the tip of the tail, with crepe paper, use the darker of the two blues and cut seven pieces 25 cm (10 in) × 8 cm (3 in) and roll the sides to

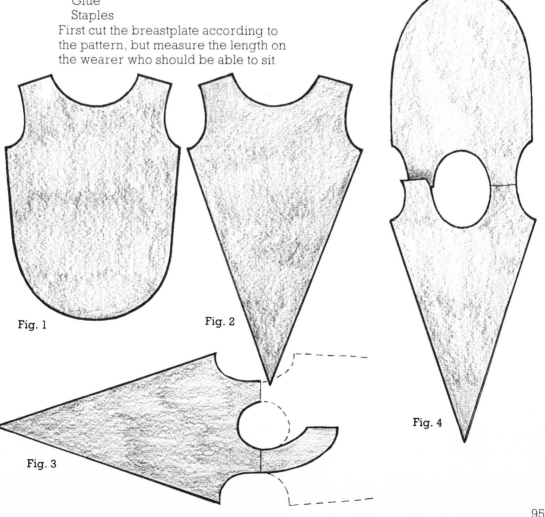

Fig. 1

Fig. 2

Fig. 3

Fig. 4

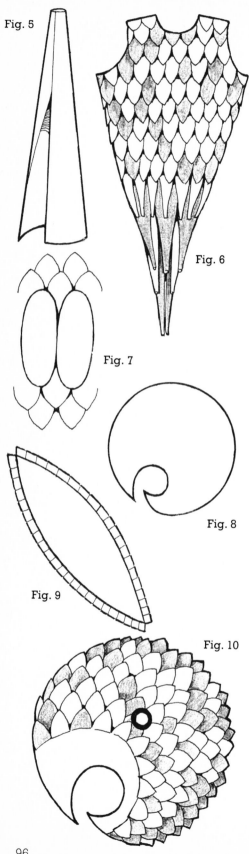

Fig. 5

Fig. 6

Fig. 7

Fig. 8

Fig. 9

Fig. 10

form a conical shape and secure the tips with glue (Fig. 5). Apply glue to the entire surface of the back and tail, or a portion at a time if the glue is a quick drying type, and attach the tail feathers.

All the other feathers are in the more conventional shape of a pointed oval measuring 12·5 cm (5 in) × 8 cm (3 in) and require a slight curling so that the layers lift off the surface and are thus clearly defined. Work the entire surface to the shoulder by adding each feather separately, using first the royal blue, and then the yellow before reaching the red on the shoulders (Fig. 6).

The front of the bird is entirely red and is also worked from the tip of the shoulder adding feathers one at a time. To conceal the join at the shoulder use oval pieces which are moulded at both ends (Fig. 7).

The dramatic mask is made by cutting two large discs adjusted to fit the head into which are cut the outline of the beak (Fig. 8). Then measure the length of the circumference and cut a strip of cover paper which starts and finishes with a point, but reaches a width of 8 cm (3 in) in the centre. Cut an extra 2·5 cm (1 in) all round for the turnings. These two areas should be cut into tabs at regular intervals along the entire length (Fig. 9), folded over and coated with glue. Place the strip between the two mask sides and use the glued tabs to hold it all together.

Paint a good thick covering of white and black on the beak and eye on both sides, and cut a notch out of the back of the gusset strip at the point, so that it can be put on and off with comparative ease. Use slightly smaller feathers than those on the body and attach red ones all over the strip between the two sides, working from the front to the back. Fill in the sides with white feathers, starting at the edge and working into the centre (Fig. 10).

Any costume of this complexity is certain to be time-consuming but all the time is well-invested. It is bound to cause considerable success whenever such a costume is required.

Dolls

These little, historical figures are a delight to make in paper and the variety of material available is an invitation itself. The range of paper from the flexible crepe papers to the stiff cards, with the additional decorations possible in flocked, metallic and other printed papers, make it possible to produce dolls of all kinds. Whether you prefer to make perfect reproductions of period figures or stylized versions, or a fairy doll, perhaps, for the Christmas Tree. The fragility of the papers make these dolls collectors' pieces as they are not robust enough to withstand the rigours of play. This is a fascinating side of papercraft, the dolls can be interesting to make, each one using relatively small amounts of material. Often the addition of a new piece of paper can inspire a new face for the collection.

Fairy Doll

At Christmas time it is a tradition in some families to place a star at the top of their Christmas Tree, but with others it is the fairy doll which commands the prime position there. A charming character to make, the layers of frill in her tutu enhance the figure at the top of the branches. She is made, like all the dolls, on a wire frame which is bound many times with crepe paper until the required proportions are achieved. This enables her to have flexible limbs, especially her legs, which can be entwined around the top of the tree.

To make the fairy doll you will need:—
 7 stem wires 25 cm (10 in) long
 Pink crepe paper 2·5 cm (1 in) wide
 White crepe paper for her tutu
 Silver foil crepe for her dress
 Tinsel
 Puffball 6·5 cm (2½ in) diameter
 Red sequins to decorate her dress
 Yellow crepe paper 2·5 cm (1 in) wide
 Binding wire
 Paint and glue

Cover five of the stem wires with pink crepe paper, bend the ends over to secure the paper and make the feet and hands. Then twist the wires together to form the body, legs and arms. Loop the fifth wire round the puffball and twist it together to form the neck, before adding it to the body by twisting it to the rest (Fig. 1).

Remembering that the fairy is a little girl, add sufficient wrappings to build up the body shape and tummy (Fig. 2). Cut a little rectangular piece of crepe paper 5 cm (2 in) × 1 cm (½ in) for her panties and glue them into position (Fig. 3).

Then cut out three more rectangles 7·5 cm (3 in) × 25 cm (10 in) with the crinkles running across the strips. Stretch out all of the long sides so that they are frilly and paint the edges with red paint. Then place one on top of another so that the layers are 1 cm (½ in) below each other, and fold them all over horizontally at the same time. Make the fold so that the distance between each frill remains the same when all the six layers are visible (Fig. 4).

Open the fold very slightly so that the piece of binding wire can be inserted into the fold before gathering the frills together as tightly as possible. Apply a liberal layer of glue around the hips of the fairy doll, and hold the frills in position until the glue dries. Twist the ends of the wire together as tightly as possible (Fig. 5). Separate the frills to reveal undulating edges.

The covering layer of the skirt is made with foil crepe paper which is cut to a rectangle 5 cm (2 in) × 22·5 cm (9 in) with the crinkles running across the piece. Fold the longest side over 2 cm ($\frac{1}{2}$ in) and insert a piece of binding wire in the fold, secure it with glue all along and leave to dry before gathering it together. Cut the unfolded edge to tiny points (Fig. 6) and shape them slightly so that they curl upwards at each tip. Place in position on top of the frills and add a little glue to hold it in place.

Complete the dress covering by cutting a bodice shape to fit the remainder of the body, remembering to shape the top of the bodice up over the bust line (Fig. 7). Wrap this round her and secure with glue.

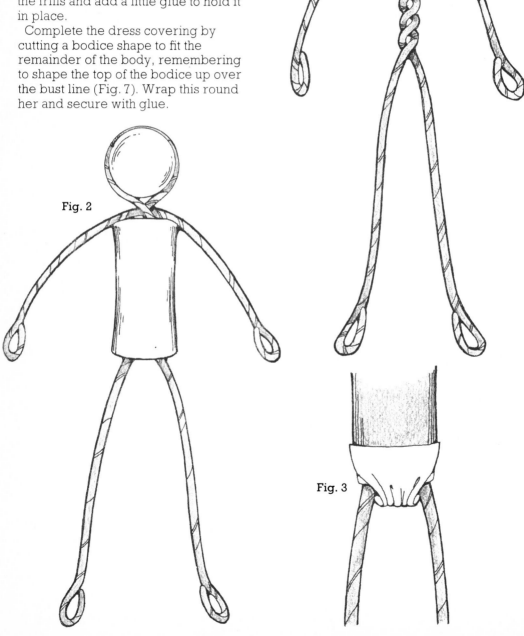

Fig. 1

Fig. 2

Fig. 3

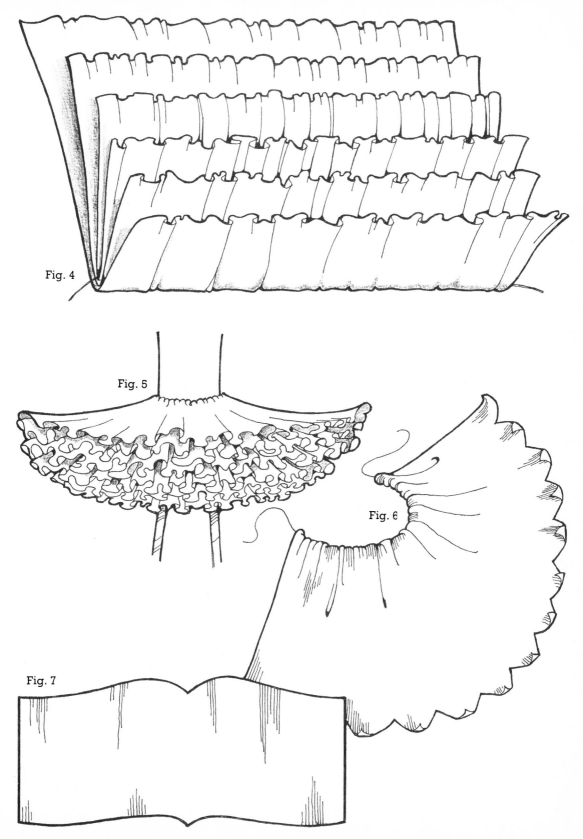

Fig. 4

Fig. 5

Fig. 6

Fig. 7

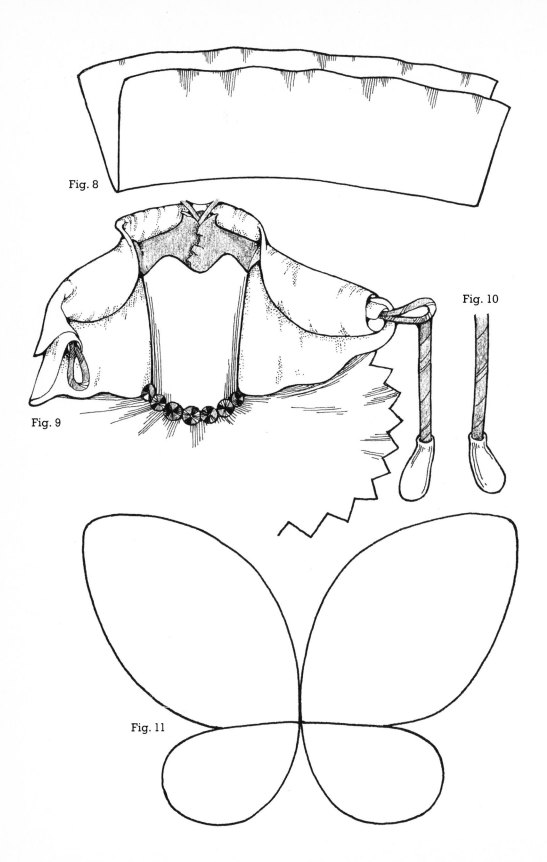

Fig. 8

Fig. 10

Fig. 9

Fig. 11

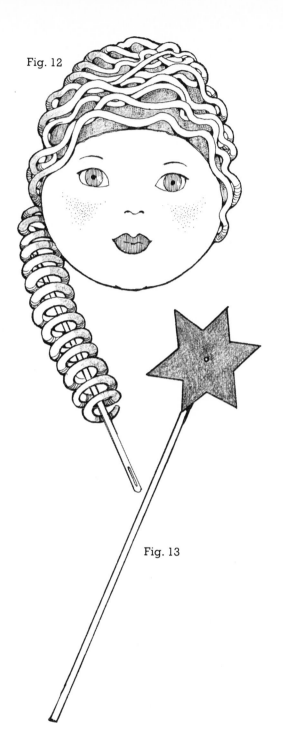

Fig. 12

Fig. 13

A short cloak draped across her arms covers the thin wires there, imitating the shape of the wings behind. This is made from a piece of the white crepe paper measuring 6·5 cm (2½ in) × 16 cm (6½ in) with the crinkles running across the strip. Both edges require a thin line of red paint along them, and then the whole piece is folded over lengthways so that the edges lie one above the other (Fig. 8). Attach the cloak by coiling it over each arm and securing it with a little glue, allowing it to drape loosely behind her (Fig. 9).

Her feet, as they are to be lost among the branches of the tree and used for security, are simply the wires covered with tiny pieces of foil crepe for shoes. These may require a little glue for security (Fig. 10).

Her wings are made by covering two lengths of stem wires with white crepe paper and then shaping each one into a wing shape on either side (Fig. 11). They are covered with tinsel and attached with glue to the centre of her back.

Her facial features are simply painted onto the puffball, but as it is made with compressed tissue paper it is advisable to use the paint as dry as possible to avoid any running.

To make her hairstyle, first cover the hair area with a tiny piece of yellow crepe paper and secure it with glue, then make some paper twine from the same coloured yellow crepe paper and wind it round a cocktail stick very tightly before releasing it to attach as undulating waves and curves. For the ringlet the paper twine is made over a piece of binding wire so that it will retain the shape of the corkscrew (Fig. 12).

Finally she has a wand, which is a small remaining piece of stem wire covered with white paper twine and with a star-shaped sequin glued to the the top (Fig. 13). The other sequins are added at the appropriate places to give additional sparkle to her dress. Completely made with paper, this little fairy doll is ready to take her place on the top of the Christmas Tree.

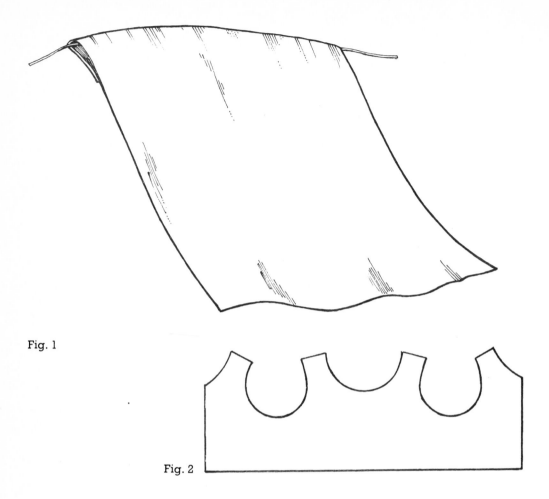

Fig. 1

Fig. 2

Kate Greenaway Doll

The pleasant pastime of making paper dolls need not be restricted to Christmas, as there are many other designs which are interesting to make, both simple and complicated. They are all equally rewarding. Present day and fantasy dresses can be made, but there is a wealth of design to be derived from historical fashions. With the example of the suggestions that are shown here it is possible to adapt the processes and reproduce many variations.

To start with the simplest, this doll is from the age of Kate Greenaway. The flattering high waistlines, with frilled hems and wide sashes, accompanied by large mob-caps, lend themselves to reproduction in crepe paper.

To make the Kate Greenaway doll you will need:—
A shaped body with arms, legs and head made with a puffball, similar to the fairy doll
Yellow double crepe paper for the dress, hat and bag
Dark red flocked paper for the accessories
Brown single crepe paper for the hair
Binding wire
Start with the skirt, and cut a piece of the double crepe paper 13 cm (4½ in) × 25 cm (6 in) with the crinkles running across the piece of paper. Stretch out one of the long sides to produce a frilly edge, and fold the other over

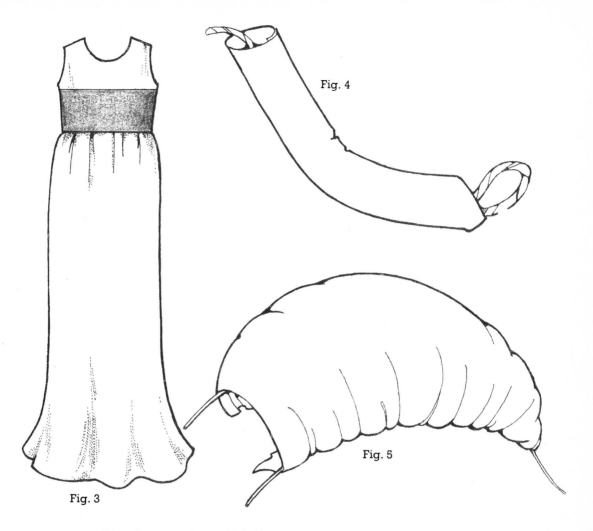

Fig. 4

Fig. 5

Fig. 3

1 cm ($\frac{1}{2}$ in). Insert a piece of binding wire into the fold (Fig. 1), secure the fit and join the open overlap with glue and leave to dry. Gather it together until it fits snugly around the doll above the waist position by twisting the ends of the wire together, and secure with glue.

The bodice is also cut from a piece of double crepe paper according to the pattern (Fig. 2) allowing room for the neck and arm holes. This will have to be adjusted to fit the particular doll that is to wear it. Place it in position and secure with glue.

Cover the area where the two papers meet with a strip of dark red flocked paper which should be at least 2 cm ($\frac{1}{2}$ in) wide, and be attached to form the high waistband (Fig. 3). Measure the

arms and cut a small piece of the double crepe paper so that it covers the arms snugly like a tube, and then make an identical one for the other arm. These sleeves are most elegant if they have an irregular hem line that tapers to a point over each hand (Fig. 4). Overlap the paper arm coverings underneath and secure with glue.

Her puffed sleeves are made from a small piece of double crepe paper 2·5 cm (1 in) × 5 cm (2 in) with the crinkles running across the strip. Make a fold along each of the long sides as small as possible, insert the binding wire, secure the fold with glue, and then gather it together when the glue has dried. Gathering on both sides of the piece of paper will produce the required puffed shape for

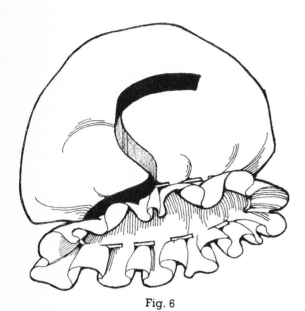

Fig. 6

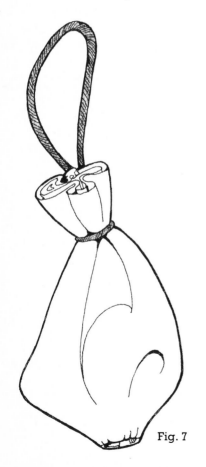

Fig. 7

the sleeves, and can be threaded into the arms and secured with glue (Fig. 5).

Round her neck there is a little choker made with a small strip of the dark red flocked paper. Make her face by painting it in the same way as the fairy doll, with very dry paint, preferably not water based. The mob cap on her head appears almost to swamp her little face but there is sufficient space around, between it and her face, for a cluster of curls and ringlets. These are made by making brown paper twine with crepe paper over binding wire and then rolling it over a needle. When released the curls can be cut off and used to curve and tumble around her face, each one attached with a little glue.

Make her mob cap by cutting a piece of double crepe paper into a circular shape 8 cm (3 in) diameter, and then stitch it with binding wire to gather the shape together approximately 0·5 cm ($\frac{1}{4}$ in) from the edge. Pull the gathering so that it fits snugly to her head, and yet allows the curls to be clearly visible (Fig. 6). The stitching is then covered with a tiny thin strip of the dark red flocked paper, which is glued into position around the cap.

Young ladies in those elegant days always carried little pochettes, and this can be made with a piece of double crepe paper 3 cm (1$\frac{1}{2}$ in) square. Make a tiny hem by folding one of the sides over, insert the binding wire and glue the hem before gathering it up into a bunch. Easing the base of the bag out a little, bind the top with binding wire allowing a small amount to frill out again above it. It is finally attached with a thin piece of brown paper twine, which is simply tied round the gathering and looped over her right wrist (Fig. 7).

She has fairly large feet which may possibly support her on their own, but it is advisable to add a third leg at the back. This is hidden by her skirt as it is underneath the layers of paper. Her shoes are simply made from a small piece of dark red flocked paper glued into position as a covering.

Victorian Doll

One of the most frequently imitated periods is the Victorian, so no group would be complete without an example from their fashions. The large flowing crinolines worn in various forms for all occasions are really easy to imitate, and with the addition of frills and a large bonnet paper dolls from the period are interesting to make.

To make the Victorian doll you will need:—
  Red single crepe paper for her
  dress and hat
  Gold foil crepe paper for the frills
  Binding wire
Make a shaped body with arms and legs and a puffball, similar to the fairy doll. Shape a mature figure with a tiny waist and add a third leg at the back for additional support.

Using the red crepe paper cut a piece 12·5 cm (5 in) × 40 cm (16 in) with the crinkles running across the paper and fold over the longest side. Insert a piece of binding wire into the fold before securing the fold with glue. When it is dry it can be gathered together to fit the waistline, but before this there are extra frills to add to the hem of the dress.

First frill the lower hem of the dress, then cut two frills from both the gold foil crepe paper and the red crepe paper 2·5 cm (1 in) wide, with the crinkles running across the strip. Stretch the edges out along the longest sides to form the frills and, as this process distorts the paper to a certain extent, leave the fitting of the length of the paper until it is ready to glue into position. As each frill is attached to the previous frill by underlapping it slightly they should all be the same length. Use the colours alternately so that each layer is clearly defined (Fig. 1).

Fig. 1

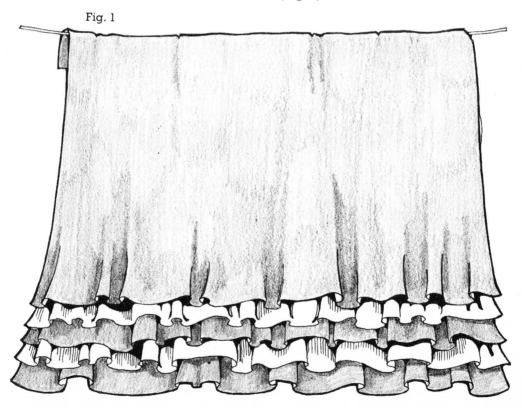

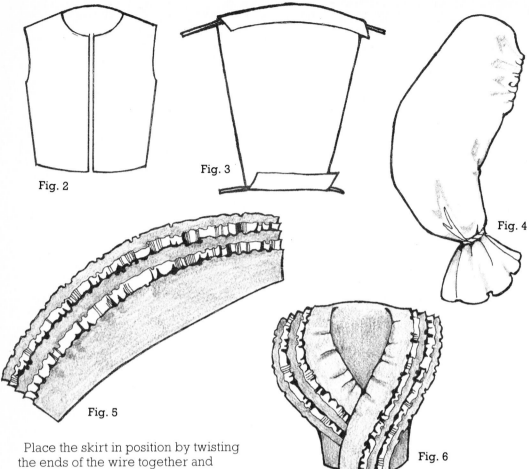

Fig. 2

Fig. 3

Fig. 4

Fig. 5

Fig. 6

Place the skirt in position by twisting the ends of the wire together and securing with glue, and also use glue to fix the overlapping join at the back.

Make the bodice by cutting a piece of red crepe paper 10 cm (4 in) × 3 cm (1¼ in) with the crinkles running the length of the paper. Fold the piece of paper in half across the width, and make a central cut from one end up to the fold, and then enlarge the cut to make a little circle for the neck (Fig. 2).

Apply a coat of glue to the entire surface and attach the bodice by overlapping the sides at the waist, and cut away the corners to make a 'V' shaped neck.

For the sleeves use the red crepe paper and cut two fan-shaped pieces which measure 5 cm (2 in) × 12·5 cm (5 in) with the crinkles running the length of the paper. Fold the short end over to make a fold (Fig. 3). Insert the binding wire before securing with

glue and gathering the pieces together. Attach this point to the shoulders and twist the wires together to control the gathering. Fix into position with glue, also run a line of glue to join the underarm seam. At the wrist simply bind the point with binding wire leaving a long frilly cuff which covers the hands (Fig. 4).

Then add an extra frill to each wrist by cutting two strips of each of the crepe papers 2 cm (¾ in) × 5 cm (2 in), joining the two together, gathering in the usual manner and fixing onto a piece of binding wire. Attach a frill to each wrist by twisting the wires together underneath.

Make a frilled collar for the bodice by using some more of the double frills that were made for the bottom of the skirt, but place them slightly closer than those on the skirt. Secure the spacing with a coating of glue on the back (Fig. 5). The strip should be at least twice as long as the measurement of the doll from waist to shoulder. Fold over the unfrilled side to enclose the gathering wire and adjust to fit the neckline, so that it is a continuous flow of frills which starts at the waist, traces the line round the neck and down again to cross over the first at the waist again (Fig. 6).

The frills may well appear too wide at the base, so they can be trimmed to echo the slim shape. It is advisable to trim all the layers so that none are lost due to the re-shaping. A twisted imitation bow finishes the bodice at the front of the waist.

Paint her face in similar fashion to the other dolls, and make her hair using brown crepe paper twine. Give her a centre parting, spiralling the hair into 'earphones' on either side (Fig. 7).

For the bonnet the skirt frill is used again, but with all the four layers filling the underside to frame the face. Glue this into position gathering it slightly so that it can fan out sufficiently (Fig. 8). Make the back by cutting a little piece of red crepe 2·5 cm (1 in) × 8 cm (3½ in) with the crinkles running across the strip. Fold one of the long sides over to form the hem and insert a piece of binding wire. Glue the hem and gather the strip together to form a little ring of gathers. Make a second fold along the length of the paper and open again to place in position at the back of the bonnet (Fig. 9). Secure with glue and cover the join with a roll of foil crepe which meets under the chin with a little bow (Fig. 10). This lady is 25 cm (10 in) tall and will happily combine with the Kate Greenaway lady, who is 20 cm (8 in) tall.

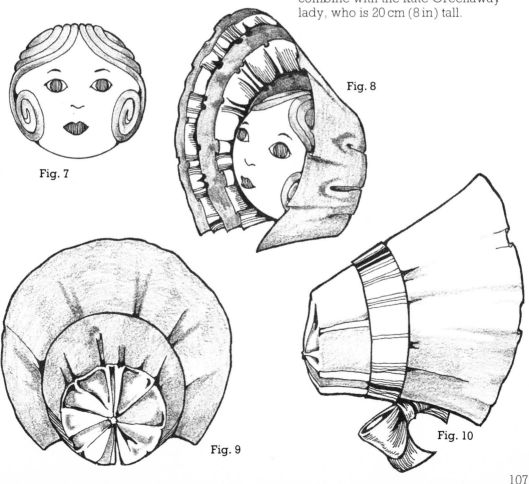

Fig. 7

Fig. 8

Fig. 9

Fig. 10

Elizabeth I Doll

There is one particularly famous lady who deserves inclusion in this group of historical period dolls, and that is Elizabeth I, who with all her jewellery adorning lavish dresses, and heavily decorated clothing made a handsome contribution to the fashions of the sixteenth century. At this time fashionable clothes became highly-tailored and uncomfortable as a contrast to the loose-fitting clothes of the Roman and medieval periods. These were usually made with rich fabrics to display their wealth and jewellery. This was always worn, for safety, and so Elizabethan clothes became elaborate jewellery boxes made of velvet and richly encrusted brocades.

She is made, like the other dolls, entirely from paper except for her jewels which are tiny beads and sequins.

To make Elizabeth I you will need:—
A shaped body with arms and legs and a puffball, made as for the fairy doll
Two extra stem wires covered with pink crepe paper
Strips of pink crepe paper 2·5 cm (1 in) wide
1 roll of double crepe paper
Foil crepe paper to cover the cloak
Flocked paper for the bodice and to line the cloak
Orange crepe paper
Strings of tiny pearls
Red sequins
6 pearls
Single white crepe paper
Glue
Binding wire
Add an extra leg to the back of the figure before commencing manufacture, and then shape two more wires so that they form a double loop on either side of the waist with the top one smaller than the lower one. These form the farthingale supports known as 'panniers' on either side (Fig. 1).

Cut a strip across the roll of double crepe paper 15 cm (6 in) wide and fold

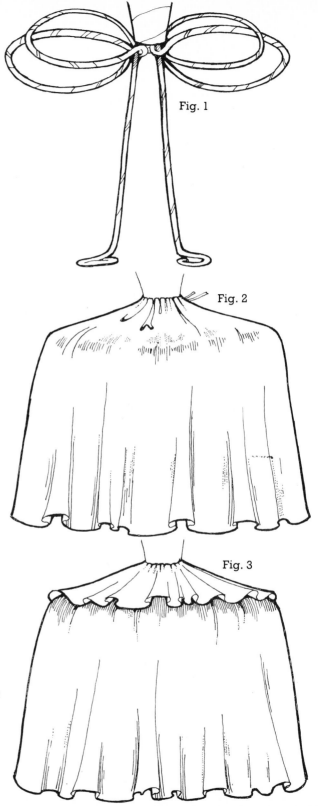

Fig. 1

Fig. 2

Fig. 3

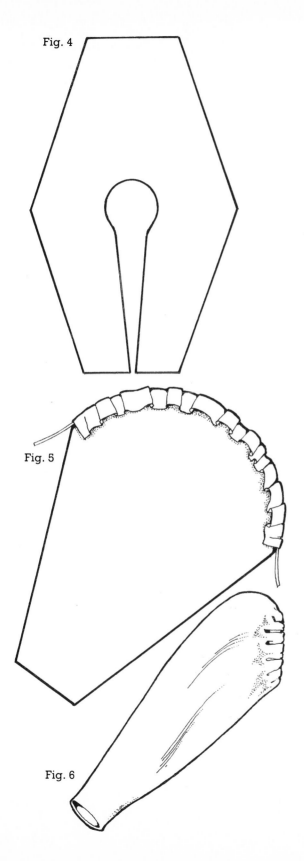

Fig. 4

Fig. 5

Fig. 6

along one of the longest sides to form a hem. Insert the binding wire and secure with glue before gathering the strip together. Place it in position round the waist adding a little glue if necessary. Arrange the skirt so that the gathers are evenly dispersed over the hoops, and trim the hem at the back and front so that it just clears the ground (Fig. 2). It is not essential to join the back because her cloak covers it later.

Measure the distance between the waist and the edge of the widest hoop and cut a strip from the roll of double crepe paper to fit. This forms the basque which is the short skirt hanging from the waistline. Fold over the longest side approximately 1 cm ($\frac{1}{2}$ in) to form a hem, insert the binding wire, glue the fold and gather the strip to fit the waist. Attach it to the waist, add a little glue if necessary, and trim the front and back so that it is parallel with the lower hem (Fig. 3).

Next make a piece for the bodice by cutting the double crepe paper into a strip 5 cm (2 in) × 10 cm (4 in) which widens to a point in the centre on both sides, with the crinkles running across the strip. Cut a slit up the centre of the front and small hole for the neck (Fig. 4). Place it in position and secure with glue.

For the sleeves cut two pieces from the double crepe which are fan-shaped, with the crinkles running lengthways, 1 cm ($\frac{1}{2}$ in) × 9 cm ($3\frac{1}{2}$ in) to 10 cm (4 in) at the top (Fig. 5). Fold as small as possible to form a hem at the top, insert the binding wire in the fold, glue and gather together. Attach to the shoulders with a little glue, twisting the ends of the wire together under the arms. Coil the sleeves round the wrist and secure with glue so that they half cover her hands (Fig. 6).

The Stomacher is the stiff bodice which is richly encrusted with jewels. It is cut from a triangular piece of dark red flocked paper 5 cm (2 in) across the top to 8 cm (3 in) to the point. Attach this to the front of the bodice with a little glue so that the point covers half of the basque, well down

Fig. 7

Fig. 8

past the natural waistline. This produces strange unbalanced proportions but it was a trend of the fashions at that time (Fig. 7).

Being a leader in fashionable clothes Queen Elizabeth I wore her ruff away from her neck, in fact from either side of her bodice. Blue starch was used at the time, but single white crepe paper is sufficient here. Cut a strip 4 cm (1½ in) × 30 cm (12 in) long and fold it in half lengthways. Insert a piece of binding wire in the fold and gather it until it fits the area it is to fill. Then attach it with glue (Fig. 8).

Behind her she trails a magnificent cloak, and this is made with foil crepe which is lined with the dark red flocked paper. Cut the foil crepe first to a rectangular shape measuring 25 cm (10 in) × 22·5 cm (9 in) with the crinkles running lengthways. Although the flocked paper is used for the lining cut the piece only 22·5 cm (9 in) square, this allows the extra area of foil crepe to make the gathering onto the shoulders.

Coat the whole surface of the back of the flocked paper and stick it to the back of the foil crepe, aligning the two together at the bottom. Fold the foil crepe 2·5 cm (1 in) down from the top and insert a wire in the fold. Secure the hem with glue and gather it

together (Fig. 9), until it fits snugly under the ruff. Fix it in position with some glue and gently crease the paper so that it is angled at the shoulders. The cloak is likely to require trimming at the two lowest points at the front sides of the hem, so that it is an equal distance from the floor all round (Fig. 10).

Her facial features are painted but remember to use the paint as dry as possible to avoid running. Make her hairstyle by covering the area with a flat piece of orange crepe paper, stretching the crinkles so that the paper snugly grips her head. Then build up her tall hairstyle with paper twine by winding it round and securing the occasional point with glue on either side. Attach one or two loops so that there is some of her hair which is not stuck entirely flat (Fig. 11). Use red designers' colours to paint a design on the skirt and sleeves, and also along the frilled edges of the ruff and basque to accentuate the outline.

Finally add the vital jewels as decorations not only on her dress where there are diamond shapes of foil crepe paper behind some of the sequins, but on her hair and round her neck, where there is also the long double layer of pearls that she always wore.

Fig. 9

Fig. 10

Fig. 11

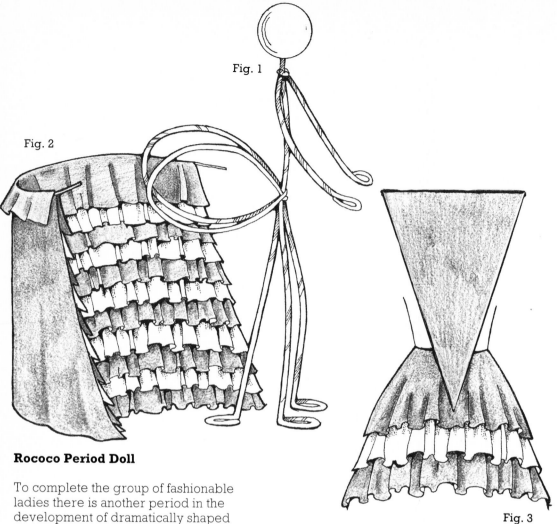

Fig. 1

Fig. 2

Fig. 3

Rococo Period Doll

To complete the group of fashionable
ladies there is another period in the
development of dramatically shaped
skirts. Panniers of wire retained by
ribbon streamers supported not only
farthingales but bustles too. These
draperies must have been extremely
cumbersome, but trailed elegantly
behind as the ladies drifted around.
Although the shape was indeed
fashionable in the eighteenth century
in the Rococo era, it also made a
dramatic reappearance a hundred
years later in what was called the 'new
Rococo' or 'the bustle of the
Seventies'. This particular lady is
wearing a red and white frilled skirted
dress of the original style.

To make the Rococo Lady you will
need:—
    1 body with arms and legs, and a
    puffball head retained by a loop of
    covered wire

Red single crepe paper for the
dress
White single crepe paper for the
dress
White double crepe paper for the
bodice and fan
Red flocked paper for the stomacher
and bows
Brown single crepe paper for her
hair
Binding wire
Glue
Extra covered stem wires for
pannier and supporting leg

Make an extra leg and attach it to the
back of the waist for stability. Make a
pannier by shaping two of the stem
wires into loops, one of which is larger
than the other, and fix it to the body by
twisting it round the waist (Fig. 1).

112

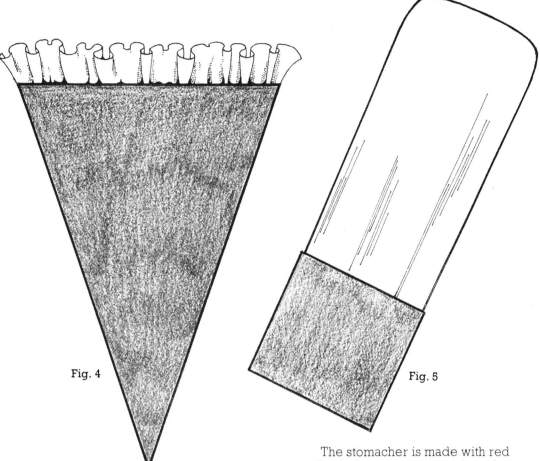

Fig. 4

Fig. 5

Make the front of the skirt by cutting a piece of single red crepe paper 20 cm (8 in) × 25 cm (10 in) with the crinkles running the 20 cm (8 in) direction. The whole of the surface is covered with frills and these are alternate layers of white and red. For each one cut a strip across the roll of either red or white 2·5 cm (1 in) wide and stretch the long side out to frill the edges. Attach each layer 1 cm ($\frac{1}{2}$ in) above the previous one using a different colour each time. There are sixteen frills altogether.

Fold the top of the skirt over 2·5 cm (1 in) from the edge as a hem, insert a piece of binding wire into the fold and secure with glue, then gather (Fig. 2). Attach to the waist by twisting the ends together. The skirt will not cover the pannier but this is not essential as the bustle covers it later.

The stomacher is made with red flocked paper, so cut a triangular piece measuring 4 cm (1$\frac{1}{2}$ in) across the top, and 6·5 cm (2$\frac{1}{2}$ in) deep. Attach it to the front of the bodice with a little glue, allowing the point to overlap the top frill of the skirt (Fig. 3).

Inside the neckline there is a demure double frill which nestles underneath. Barely visible this little frill is cut from a piece of single white crepe paper 4 cm (1$\frac{1}{2}$ in) × 1 cm ($\frac{1}{2}$ in) which is folded in half lengthways and frilled along both the long edges (Fig. 4).

Next cover the sleeves with double crepe paper by cutting two pieces 10 cm (4 in) × 3 cm (1 in) with rounded tops. Cut two contrasting cuffs from the red crepe paper 2·5 cm (1 in) × 3 cm (1$\frac{1}{4}$ in) and glue them to the sleeves (Fig. 5). Roll the pieces into tubes and secure the overlapping join with glue, then slip over the arms and hold them in position by applying a little glue to the shoulders.

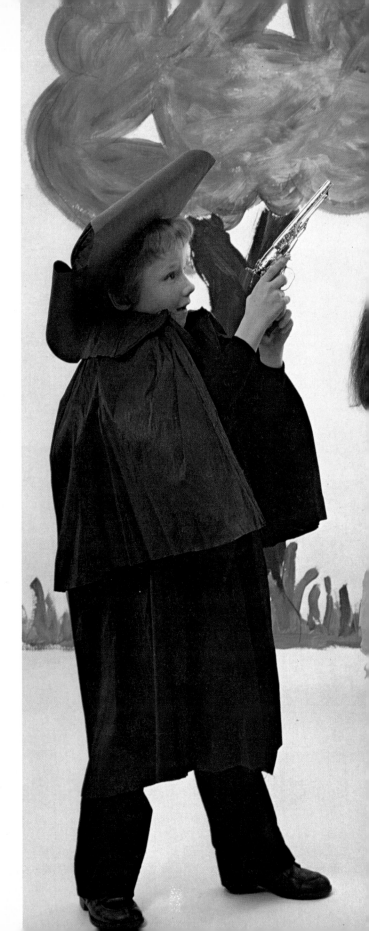

From left to right: Highwayman, Hawaiian girl, Little Miss Muffet and the Parrot.

For special occasions it is well worth the time and effort required to make these complete costumes as the expressions on the children's faces show.

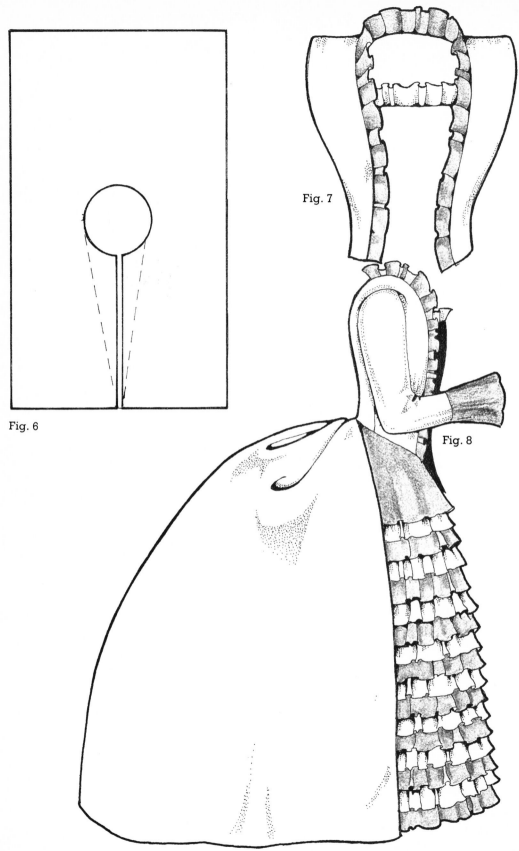

Fig. 6

Fig. 7

Fig. 8

116

Fig. 9

Fig. 10

Then, using the double crepe paper again, cut a rectangular piece for the jacket 5 cm (2 in) × 12·5 cm (5 in) and make a cut up the centre. Enlarge this cut to a ring for the neckline, cutting the corners at the front of the neck away (Fig. 6). Make a tiny red frill and attach it to the inside of the neck so that only a line of red is visible. Fix the jacket over the body and overlap the sides, securing with glue (Fig. 7).

Her bustle is made with a layer of white single crepe paper with a lining of red single crepe paper which is revealed by the way the material is draped at the sides. Cut both pieces the same size, 18 cm (8 in) × 30 cm (12 in) with the crinkles running the length of the 30 cm (12 in) side.

Use both layers as if they were one,

and make a double pleat into the back of the waist and secure it with glue. Then stretch out the crinkles until the bustle forms a domed shape, and reaches the ground at the furthest point from the centre back (Fig. 8). Fold back the corners on either side and, making a tiny pleat, attach with glue and add a flocked paper bow shape (Fig. 9). Do this on both sides so that the red lining is well displayed.

Paint her facial features and add her hair, which is made entirely with paper twine. This is made over binding wire and then rolled into ringlets over a cocktail stick (Fig. 10). Finally, complete her with a fan which stands erect in her hair, and one which hangs from a paper twine ring in her hand.

117

From left to right: Victorian Doll, Queen
Elizabeth I Doll, Kate Greenaway Doll and
the Rococo Period Doll.

A collection of period dolls can be
enhanced by use of toning colour schemes
and effective display.

Noah's Ark

This stylized version of Noah's Ark is one which lends itself to recreation in paper. The ark can be obtained from shops in kit form and, although it is cheating somewhat to use a ready-cut and printed shape, it will most probably come as a welcome time-saver after all the animals have been assembled. If, however, you prefer to make the ark yourself the following instructions will create the correct shape.

You will need:—

    Stiff white paper or card
    Good sharp cutting tool
    Glue and paints

Cut two boat shapes for the hull 35 cm (14 in) × 8 cm (3 in), and mark on these the wooden slats to run along the sides. In this model the card was painted a uniform brown and the boards and nails drawn with a brown felt-tip. Cut a trap door to open downwards as a gangplank for the animals to disembark, and a large double door to store all the occupants inside when they are not in use. Join the shapes at the bow and the stern, and leave to dry.

Next cut the deck shape which should have straight sides, tapered to a point at either end. This should be 30 cm (12 in) × 10 cm (4 in) and have additional tabs to bend down and fix to the sides. Mark this in the same way as the hull making the boards appear to run the length of the deck. When the shape is coloured, fix it into position joining the tabs to the sides of the boat so the level of the deck is slightly below that of the sides.

The cabin is made by cutting a shape from the paper which is to form all four sides in one piece with the tab on the last side for assembly and a tab on each side for fixing the roof. The height of the building is 7 cm (2¾ in), the length of the long wall 11·5 cm (4½ in), and the short 8 cm (3 in). Score the lines which form the corners of the cabin and fold each one. Apply glue to the tab and fix the cabin into shape and leave to dry. *Continued on page 128.*

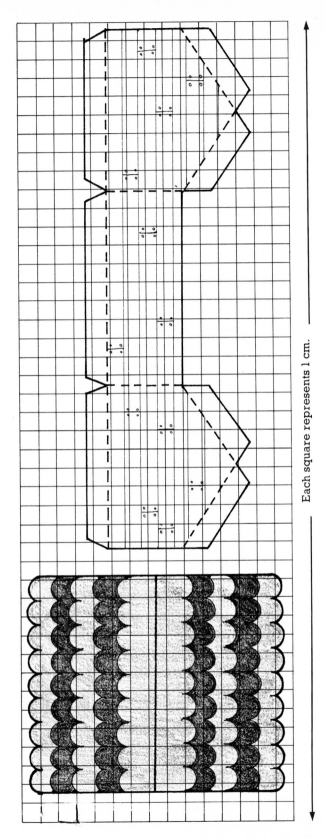

Each square represents 1 cm.

Each square represents 1 cm.

Both the animals and the ark are simple
enough for children to make themselves
and inspire hours of imaginative play.

Use this attractive arrangement of flowers to brighten a dark corner on an occasional table or special stand. Paper flower arrangements are particularly useful in winter when cut flowers are scarce and wither quickly in centrally heated rooms.

126

The roof measures 11·5 cm (4½ in) × 10·5 cm (4¼ in) and is scored along the centre and folded to form the ridge before attaching with a little glue on the tabs on the side of the cabin. Cut a window out of each side and then a large doorway out of the back, so that the animals may be easily moved in and out of the cabin. Paint the roof and walls realistically.

Apply a liberal amount of glue all along the bottom edge of the cabin and place it in position on the deck. The model can be completed by placing it onto the sea, which is simply a piece of blue, stiff paper. This could, of course, be painted just like everything else before gluing the ark into position. This model has already 'landed' on hills made from green paper, backed with stiff card.

The animals can be drawn from the enormous wealth of species in the animal kingdom. Scale plays an important part, but there can be a certain amount of artists' licence to make, for example, a small animal like the tortoise, be seen when included in the same ark as an elephant. These animals are all made from coloured art paper, which is similar in weight to heavy cartridge paper and, in fact, where the white is required, cartridge paper has been used.

Use a double layer of two toning shades of paper. This is sealed with Spray Mount from an aerosol, but in the absence of this piece of equipment a smooth even layer of glue spread as thinly as possible will be a perfect substitute. Select and cut out several chosen animals to use as templates. Cut four of each shape remembering to turn the template over for two of the four so that they are actually mirrored, and consequently ensure that the same colour is on the outside of both members of the pair. The following animals have been used for this ark: elephant, giraffe, lion, hippopotamus, horse, polar bear, goat, ostrich, dog, hedgehog, tortoise and duck, but of course there are many which have been left out. The patterns for all of these can be traced from the book if desired.

A ring of paper in one of the colours from each animal has been assembled and placed between the animal outlines. This is glued between the layers and acts to make the animals three-dimensional.

An ark of this kind filled with assorted pairs of animals will give relatively inexpensive hours of playtime for the children. It is especially suitable as a toy as, naturally, if there is any damage due to over-use it is not difficult to replace the part with a new one.

Flowers

One of the most charming forms of paper decorations is a floral one. There are many different sources of inspiration for this instantly recognisable art form. Whether they are the very simplest in design, or intensely intricate, flowermaking is an absorbing pastime which can grow into a fascinating hobby.

Many, varied demands are bound to be made on the successful flowermaker, from decorating floats for carnivals, and large halls for parties and special occasions, to tiny posies for bridesmaids to carry or to wear in their hair.

Flowers have, for centuries, been traditional gifts and now in sophisticated form of a bouquet they are welcomingly received by many a celebrity. Flowers, in their simplicity, make delightful ornamental additions to gifts, hats, or frames.

Vase of Flowers

This china vase (page 126) was a particularly favourite shape of Constance Spry's and is a delight to arrange, displaying the flowers as an informal array of mixed flora. The soft hydrangea colourings intermingle gently with a little silver, which gives a subtle sparkle.

White Lily

> White double crepe paper 23 cm (9 in) × 13 cm (5 in)
> Green double crepe paper 10 cm (4 in) × 13 cm (5 in)
> Puffball or bead 2·5 cm (1 in) diameter
> Stem and binding wire
> Binding tape
> Glue

Wind the binding tape around the stem until this is completely covered. Apply a little glue to the tip of the wire and secure this inside the puffball.

Cut eight pointed oval petals from the double crepe 2·5 cm (1 in) × 10 cm (4 in) and three leaves of similar size and shape from the green crepe (Fig. 1). Bind the petals individually to the stem just below the puffball, arranging them in two layers to encircle the centre. They should not overlap.

Trim away all the material below the binding and cover the stem with tape again, adding the leaves at intervals in the process (Fig. 2).

When the flower is complete hold it at the binding point and curl all the petals outwards (Fig. 3). Finish the leaves by giving them the same treatment.

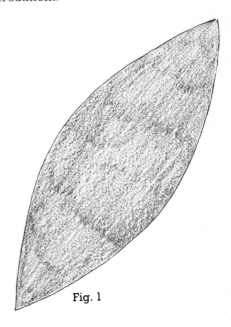

Fig. 1

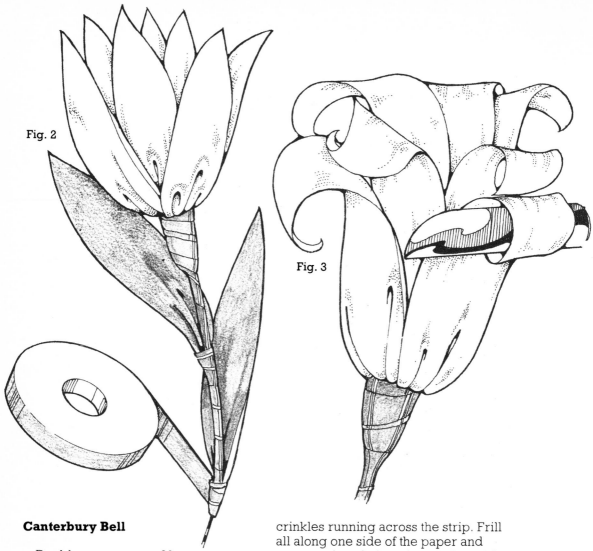

Fig. 2

Fig. 3

Canterbury Bell

Double crepe paper 23 cm
(9 in) × 13 cm (5 in)
Single crepe paper in toning colour
15 cm (6 in) × 15 cm (6 in)
Puffball or bead 2·5 cm (1 in)
diameter
Stem wire
Binding wire
Binding tape

Cover the stem with binding tape.
Apply a little glue to the top and
secure it inside the puffball. Cut a
square piece of crepe paper 6·5 cm
(2½ in) across, stretch the centre out a
little and place it over the puffball,
gathering the loose edges tightly into
the stem with binding wire (Fig. 1).

Next, cut a strip of single crepe 15 cm
(6 in) long and 8 cm (3 in) wide with the
crinkles running across the strip. Frill
all along one side of the paper and
squeeze the whole strip together; this
will pleat the frills. Bind this strip at the
same binding point as the puffball
covering, and arrange the frill so that
it encircles the ball once.

Using the double crepe paper, cut
four heart-shaped petals, each with a
short stem, 5 cm (2 in) × 10 cm (4 in).
Shape these by stretching out the
crinkles in the centre to form a cup
shape, rolling the curved tops
outwards (Fig. 2). Join the petals to the
stem individually, attaching each one
with binding wire so that it overlaps
the previous one and the four are
evenly spaced in their final positions.

Remove all the material below the
binding and cover the join and stem
again with binding tape (Fig. 3).

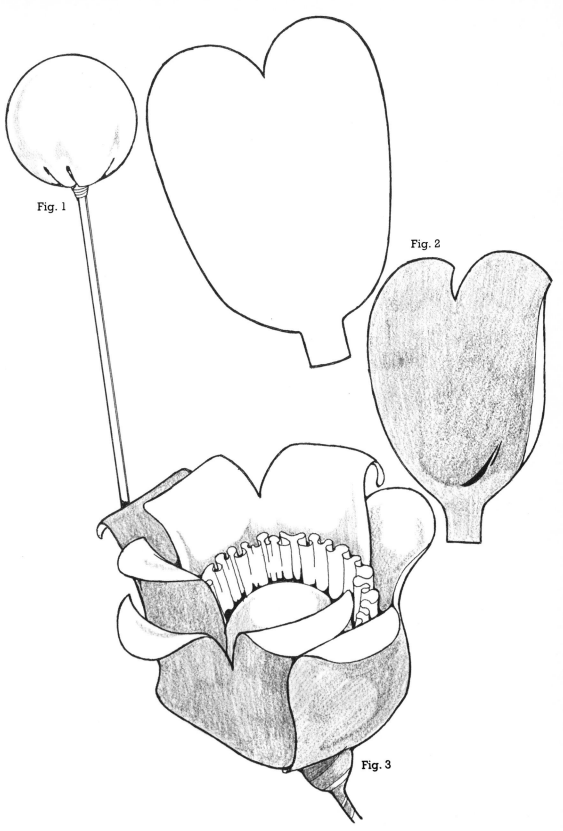

Fig. 1

Fig. 2

Fig. 3

Double Bells

Three silver pearls diameter 8 mm
($\frac{3}{8}$in)
Foil crepe paper 15 cm (6 in) × 20 cm
(8 in)
Stem wire
Binding wire
Binding tape

Thread each pearl onto a piece of
binding wire and secure the position
of each one by twisting the ends of the
wire tightly together. This traps the
pearl in the loop at the top and forms a
stem. Join the three together by
twisting the bottom of the stems,
allowing the tops to separate at
various heights. Bind the pearls to the
top of the stem wire, allowing the
pearl stems to stand 5 cm (2 in) above
the flower stem (Fig. 1).

Fold the piece of foil crepe paper
across the crinkles one-third of the
way down, then fold the long side back
so that the raw edges meet, forming a
concertina fold of three layers. Make
another fold by turning down the top
layer again so that the two open edges
are together. This will make two
visible folds on one side and one on
the other (Fig. 2).

Frill out the folded edges a little so
that they stand away from the rest of
the paper, then roll the whole piece
round so one end slots into the other to
form a tube. Place the tube over the
pearls and gather the open edges into
the pearl stem binding and secure in
the normal way with binding wire
(Fig. 3). This may squash the tube
around the binding area, so ease the
paper open again to make the
required bell shape.

The proportions of the material can
be reduced for smaller bells. A spray
of bells makes a charming variation;
each bell is made on a separate stem,
and joined to the main stem
afterwards.

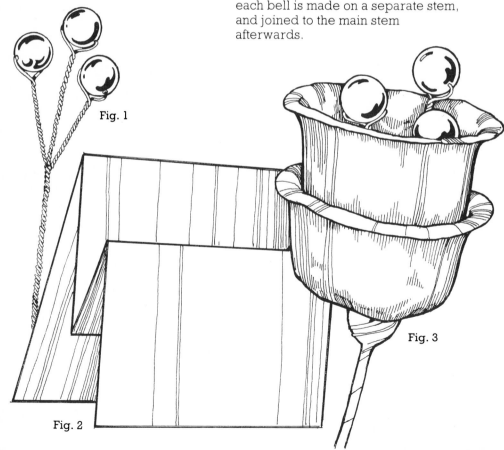

Fig. 1

Fig. 2

Fig. 3

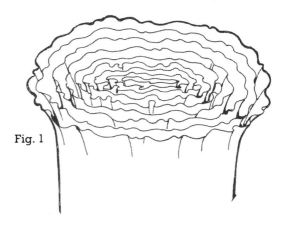

Fig. 1

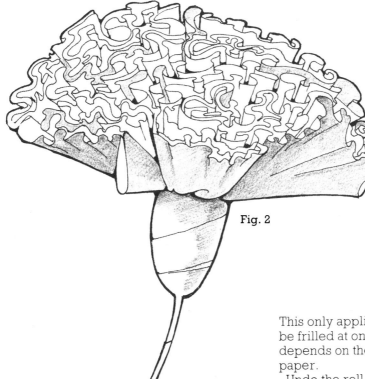

Fig. 2

Carnation

Single crepe paper 8 cm (3 in) wide,
cut across the bottom of the roll
Stem wire
Binding wire
Binding tape

Frill all along one side of the crepe
paper which, like the chrysanthemum,
will be much easier to handle if it is
kept intact in the original roll (Fig. 1).

This only applies if all the layers can
be frilled at once and this in turn
depends on the strength of the crepe
paper.

Undo the roll, gather the whole strip
together and squeeze the unfrilled
side together, so that it can be bound
to the stem. This flower requires very
firm handling and tight binding. Cover
the join and the stem with binding
tape.

The flower head should spring open
by itself if the layers were separated
before they were gathered up. If this
was not done it is not too difficult to
separate the layers once the flower is
complete. The final effect to aim for is
a dome of clearly visible frills (Fig. 2).

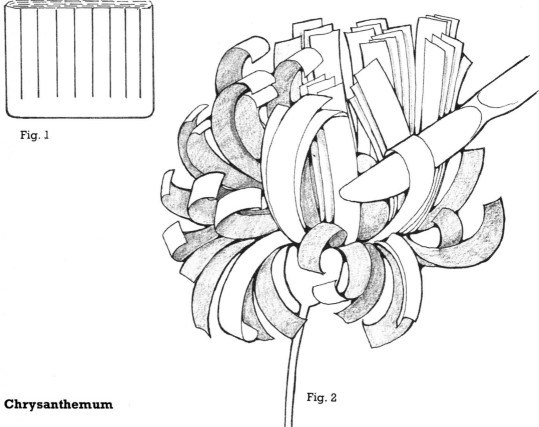

Fig. 1

Fig. 2

Chrysanthemum

Pink single crepe paper 8 cm (3 in)
wide, cut across the bottom of the
roll
Puffball or bead 2·5 cm (1 in)
diameter
Stem wire
Binding wire
Binding tape
Glue

The easiest way to obtain the long strip
of paper is to cut straight across the
bottom of the roll of crepe paper. This
will also have the advantage of
ensuring that the grain goes the right
way, that is, across the strip. It may
also be easier to work with the strip
still rolled up and complete the flower
with it like that.

Having acquired the right sized piece
of crepe paper, make cuts into it at
regular intervals leaving 2 cm ($\frac{3}{4}$ in)
intact with no cuts (Fig. 1). The petals
should now resemble a comb. Cover
the stem wire with binding tape and

apply a little glue to secure the
puffball on the top.

Gather the uncut side of the crepe
paper and bind this tightly with wire to
the stem just below and around the
puffball. Because of the large amount
of paper to be bound in, the area
round the join is sure to be bulky but
this can be kept as compact as
possible by very tight binding.
Complete the flower by covering the
binding and stem with tape.

Hold the flower firmly at the point of
binding, (this is just a precaution in
case the binding is not quite tight
enough to hold the petals in place
whilst they are being curled), and
using a blunt knife curl each of the
petals separately (Fig. 2). This should
result in an informal profusion of
tumbling petals.

Rose

White single crepe paper 8 cm
(3 in) × 75 cm (30 in)
Puffball 2·5 cm (1 in) diameter
Stem wire
Binding wire
Binding tape
Glue

Cover the stem with tape and glue the tip into position inside the puffball. Cut the crepe paper into fifteen rounded petal shapes 5 cm (2 in) × 4·5 cm (1¾ in) with the crinkles running from top to bottom of each one (Fig. 1).

Shape the centre of the petals by easing out the creases to form a cup shape, then curl the tops out a little to complete the curve (Fig. 2). Make a small dart in the base of each one. This helps to keep the petals together and the finished flower intact.

Start binding the first petal to the stem just below the puffball and continue to add the remainder overlapping each slightly with the previous one until the flower is fully assembled with all the petals (Fig. 3). Trim away all the materials below the binding and cover the stem with tape.

During the assembly of the other roses, variations are bound to occur and interesting combinations of sizes of flowers can be made by simply altering the quantity of petals.

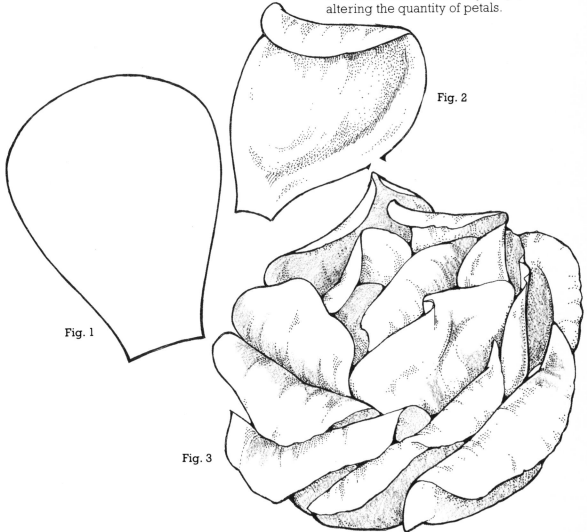

Fig. 1

Fig. 2

Fig. 3

Frilly Leaves

Green single crepe paper 10 cm
(4 in) × 15 cm (6 in)
Stem wire
Binding wire
Binding tape

Frill all along the two long sides of the
crepe paper by stretching the crinkles
apart. Fold the frilly strip in half
lengthways so that all the frills are on
the same side (Fig. 1). Insert the
binding wire into the fold and gather
the crepe paper together as tightly as
possible.

Join the two ends of the wire together
and form a loop by twisting the ends
together (Fig. 2). Try to keep the
edges of the crepe paper level, if it
has been misplaced during the
gathering it should be quite simple to
press it flat at this stage. Attach the
twisted wire to the stem wire by
placing the two together and covering
them both at once with binding tape.

When making up a spray of leaves,
vary the number of leaves according
to the area they are required to fill.
Each subsequent leaf is added in turn
below the previous one and together
they should, when assembled, form a
continuous line of leaves without much
stem showing in between them.

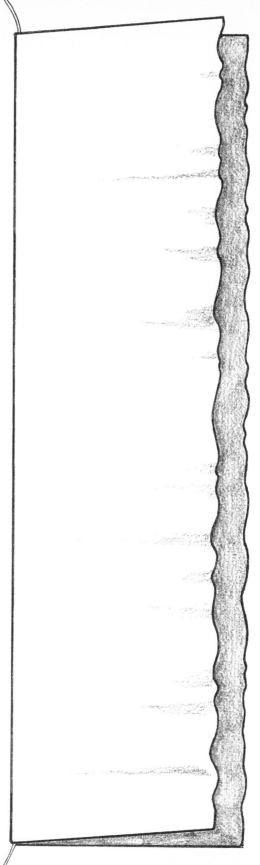

Fig. 1

136

Variegated Leaves

Green single crepe paper 15 cm
(6 in), cut from the bottom of the roll
roll
Stem wire
Bleach
Tape

Unroll the crepe, gather it loosely into
a bundle and dip the raw edges into
neat household bleach (Fig. 3). The
crinkles will expand as they do when
this paper receives similar treatment
in water. Hang up to dry.

Cut a piece 30 cm (12 in) long from
the strip and fold it in half lengthways.
Insert a stem wire in the fold and
gather the paper together twisting the
ends of the wire together to secure the
paper and create a double stem.
Cover this with tape and arrange the
papers into a complete circle and ease
the layers apart.

The leaf will appear variegated with
a green centre edged with white
irregular markings.

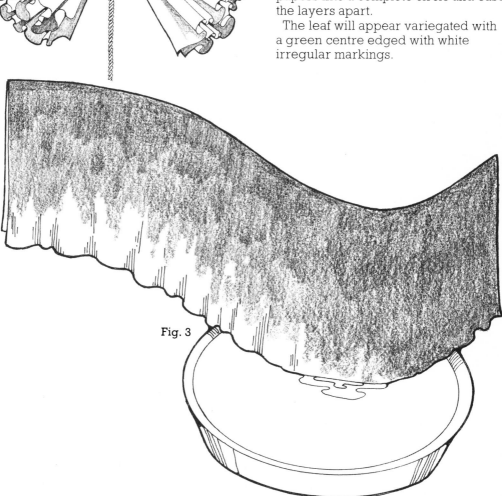

Fig. 2

Fig. 3

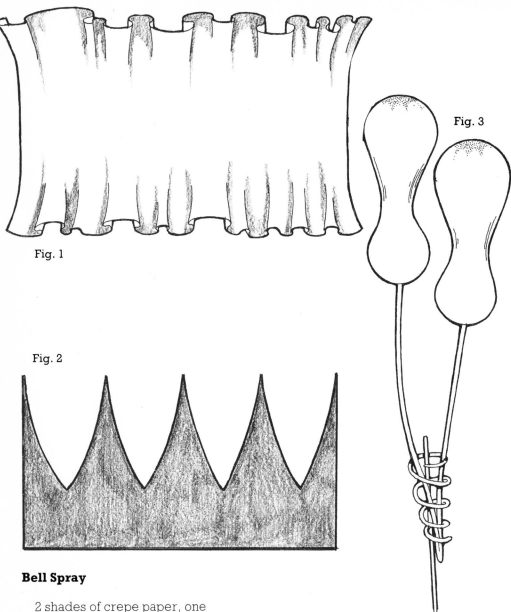

Fig. 1

Fig. 2

Fig. 3

Bell Spray

2 shades of crepe paper, one
flower-coloured, one green
Stamens
Stem wire
Binding wire

To make each little bell cut a piece of
crepe paper 13 cm (5 in) × 8 cm (3 in)
and frill along both of the short sides
(Fig. 1). This will form the petals. Now
cut a piece of green paper for the
sepals (the green outer part of the
flower), 7·5 cm (3 in) × 5 cm (1 in). Cut
one side of this into five points (Fig. 2).

To make up the flower first fold one
pair of stamens in half and bind this to
a stem (Fig. 3). Then fold the petal
piece in half so that one frill lies below
the other, and coil it round so that one
end tucks inside the other (Fig. 4).
Pinch the folded end in round the
finger forming the bell shape.

Carefully thread the petal piece onto
the stem over the stamens. Bind it
tightly then add the sepals in the same
way as the petals coiling the piece of
crepe. Make five bells altogether, and
attach them to a main stem at intervals.

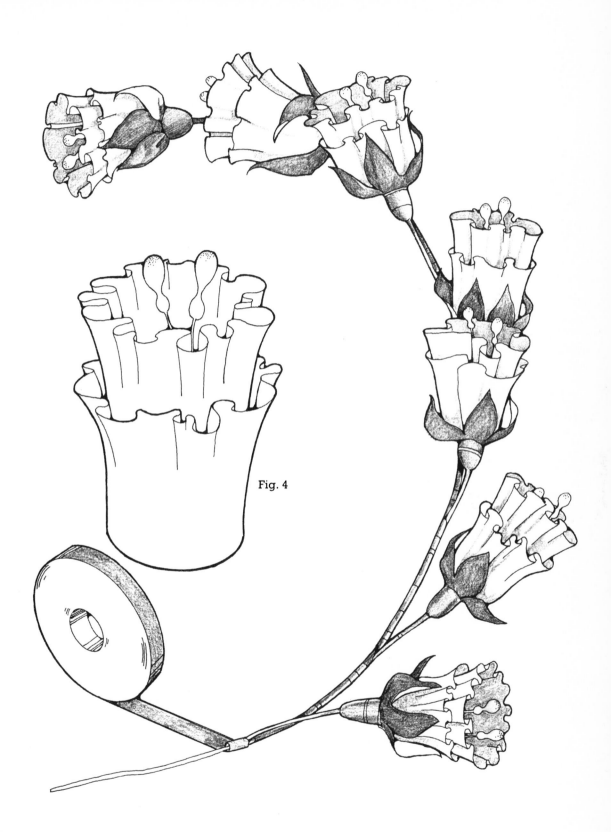

Fig. 4

139

Mexican Posy

This little posy is made from a very simple pattern shape and produced by making several identical flowers which, when joined at the same point, form a dome. The shape is enhanced by a rosette of leaves, before it is placed onto a lace posy frill, then completed by tying the handle with ribbon. This posy is suitable for a little girl to carry.

An alternative use, which is a charming Dutch custom, is to make the posy for the table and place it on a mat, a piece of mirrored glass, or in a shallow vase. A decoration of this kind is very compact and ideal for the small dinner table or occasional table. For a special occasion a small sachet of potpourri can be attached to the centre and concealed by the flowers in the dome. The compact nature of these little Mexican flowers is particularly suitable for this form of decoration, but there are several variations and other flowers can make perfectly adequate substitutes.

Daisies, for example, are refreshing for a summer table, or forget-me-nots which are the traditional flowers for the Victorian posy. Tiny rosebuds were also used by the Victorians, and were so arranged that the flowers placed in ever increasing rings were gradually shaded from dark to light. Posies of various shapes, and nosegays, were favourites of Victorian ladies and played an important part in their fashions as they were already accustomed to decorating their clothes with flowers.

Garlands

Historical Background

The garland with all its variations, whether floral or otherwise, is one of the earliest forms of decoration. Garlands, in the form of a chaplet of leaves, were worn in ancient religious ceremonies and were also placed round the shoulders of a triumphant winner in the games, a tradition which continues today.

Over the years two basic types of garlands have developed, each with their own uses. One is the floral garland and the other the chains and streamers made up of abstract shapes. The former is probably more historical and is associated with religious events whereas chains and streamers have generally been used for more festive, secular events such as carnivals.

For the milestones in family life floral garlands can be used to decorate the font for a christening, with tiny ones for the cake; garlands and floral arches can be used for wedding decorations; and Christmas invites the use of suitable material for a welcoming wreath on the door. They can be used in all sorts of formal decoration for special occasions. The Victorians had some charming customs, and their ingenious way of entwining garlands between the bannisters and over doorways are two which can be imitated. However it is unwise to invite disaster by copying their custom of decorating their mantlepieces with lavish garlands.

In contrast to the floral garlands which have the emphasis on intricate structure, streamers and paper chains are very simple in construction so that a good effect can be achieved by multiples of them tracing intricate patterns across the room. Whilst bright eye-catching colours are the most suitable for the chains and streamers, a much more gentle and subtle colour scheme can be chosen for floral garlands which will no doubt bear closer inspection.

Robert Adam and Grinling Gibbons were masters of the art of garland design whether cast in plaster or carved in wood. The Adam garlands, with their characteristic swelling in the centre or at the end of a pendant, were used in interior design and can be seen in some houses of the period as details on mantlepieces and furniture where the garland was sometimes joined into an oval. The firm of Wedgwood adopted this form of decoration for their pottery masterpieces, but the most famous garland maker of all was Grinling Gibbons whose carved wooden garlands are indeed works of art. There are some examples of his work in the Victoria & Albert Museum, where his choice of all manner of material such as cones, flowers, fruit and leaves can be seen incorporated into the garlands.

Garland Using Dried Plant Material

Garlands can be made with the influence of these great artists and the inspiration derived from an assortment of dried plant material. Although the list tells the contents exactly, each garland is an individual creation and its form will depend naturally on the material available. With all the very bright and harsh colours that are used for making paper it was not an easy task to select subtle ones which blend with the natural tones of the dried material.

However in this type of work the fewer direct contrasts the better.

Where paper is combined with dried plant material the cone or seed case provides an excellent guide to the size and shape of the petals which will combine most suitably to make a flower. The petals should echo the shape of the centre: use it as a pattern and place it on the paper and draw round it. The result will be rounded petals for a round seedhead, like for example a teazel, or pointed petals for a pointed seedhead such as the sweet chestnut.

You will need:—
15 teazels
5 long spruce cones
11 small fir cones
8 large pine cones
12 bleached sweet chestnut seed cases
6 sprays of corn
Glycerined magnolia leaves of the type available at florists
Glycerined beech leaves
Honesty
1 roll double crepe paper, pale and sage green
1 roll double crepe paper, moss and sage green
Strip of single crepe paper 12·5 cm (5 in) wide
Stem wires for each article including one for each individual leaf
Binding wire
Tape, or a strip of brown single crepe paper 2·5 cm (1 in) wide
Spray varnish

First cut the stems of the teazels to a length of 7·5 cm (3 in) and remove the prickles by drawing them between slightly open scissors. Insert the stem wire inside the hollow stem. Cut five

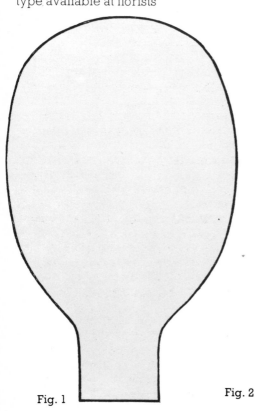

Fig. 1

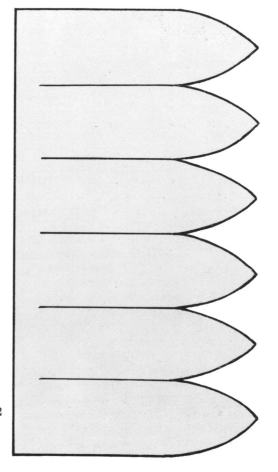

Fig. 2

Fig. 3

Fig. 4

petals from the dark green double crepe paper according to the pattern with the rounded top. They should be slightly larger than the teazel, so the actual size will naturally be dependent on that of the teazel. Make sure that the grain runs the length of the petals (Fig. 1). Mould the petals by making a cup in the centre and curving the top of them over, then attach each one by making a small pleat in the base and binding it to the stem as close to the base of the teazel as possible. Cover the stem with tape and stand in a pot while all the others are assembled.

The sweet chestnuts also have hollow stems, but it is preferable to cover the top of the stem a little way with the tape before inserting it as it will otherwise tend to twist round. Cut a strip of six petal shapes in one piece from the paler double crepe paper, making each one pointed. Once again make sure that the direction of the crinkles on the crepe paper follows the line of the petal from top to bottom (Fig. 2).

Gather the base of the petal strip and squeeze it together so that it is easier to assemble, then place it around the stem and bind it tightly just below the base of the seedhead. Cover the stem and shape the petals by easing them out from the seedhead slightly and curving the tips of the petals outwards.

The large frilly fir cone flowers are made with the single crepe paper. First cut 60 cm (24 in) from the strip of paper and cut the edges so that they are scalloped (Fig. 3). Fold the piece of paper over lengthways, not equally in half, so that the lower layer is visible beyond the top one. Place the binding wire in the fold and gather the strip together onto it.

Put the fir cone onto a wire stem by

143

making a hook in the stem wire and working it round through the lower scales; as it reaches the base it should be straightened out to form the stem. Twist the end of the wire round the stem below the fir cone. Entwine the frilly strip of petals between the scales, keeping the gathering full enough to make the petals radiate. The strip should encircle the cone twice before finishing the end by twisting it round the nearest scale (Fig. 4).

Shape the petals by stretching each one into a cup shape, this will separate the layers and echo the shape of the scales of the cone.

With the preparation of the materials almost complete, all that remains is the wiring of the dried plant material. This is done by placing a stem wire beside the dried stem so that they are level at the base, and then bending the wire over about 2·5 cm (1 in) from the base. Bind the wire around the original upright dried and wire stems together

(Fig. 5). This is the method to use for all dried material with stems, but for leaves a tiny stitch is taken in the base of the leaf before the wires are twisted together (Fig. 6).

All that remains now is to twist the materials together into the garland shapes. Start with the smallest materials and, working from the tips to the wide parts at the top or in the centre, add each additional piece of material by twisting the stems together. The completed garlands may bend easily at the end but this will, of course, be rectified when in place against the background. Flowers made with these materials will be very long lasting so that all the work is well invested in a form of decoration which will enhance any blank wall.

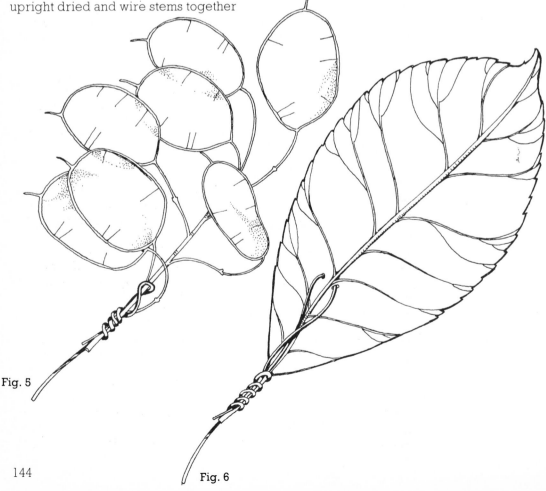

Fig. 5

Fig. 6

144

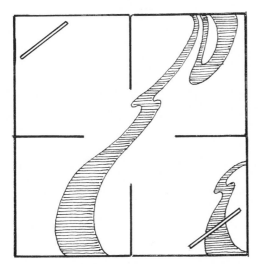

Fig. 1

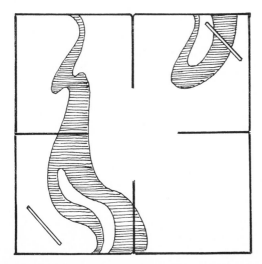

Fig. 2

Fig. 3

Paper Chains and Streamers

Paper garlands can make the most dramatic change of atmosphere, forming a colourful network made with bright streamers. There is a wealth of paper to choose from: whether stitched crepe paper, strips of any fairly strong paper for the traditional paper chain, or the elaborate expanded shapes from stamped out acetate foil film. Crepe paper has the advantage once more of being stretchable; where it is stretched at the edge it naturally forms a frill.

The simplest of all is made by cutting strips of crepe paper, approximately 8 cm (3 in) wide, from several different colours, frilling along all the long sides and then stitching with a sewing machine the entire length of the papers through all the papers at once. Then separate the layers on either side of the stitching and twist the whole streamer into a spiral.

This can be equally effective when it is made with one colour and, perhaps, tone in with another colour in the general decorations. Although an average size has been suggested, they can, of course, be varied and a combination of assorted sizes is, indeed, interesting.

For an alternative streamer the layers can be stitched in a wavy line which drifts from alternate sides in a zig-zag. Use a sewing machine for this with the top tension released. Gather the stitching until it is in a straight line again and the papers then form gathered fan shapes on alternate sides. Separate the layers of each fan. Although several can be used, it may be sufficient to use only two.

The conventional chain need hardly be mentioned, although interesting variations can be created by using acetate film as an alternative material. Assemble the rings making them various sizes, and attach them in rotation to produce a pattern.

The most effective of all the chains are the expanded shapes, which can be packed flat when out of use. A variety of shapes can be used, the

This beautiful garland combining paper
with dried plant material gives a country
atmosphere to the room.

146

simplest being the cross (Fig. 1). Cut several identical shapes from two-coloured acetate foil and staple them together at regular points (Figs. 2 and 3). When pulled apart an intriguing pattern is formed.

In addition to these, a garland can be made by attaching looped bows to alternate sides of a flat strip (Fig. 4). This is very effective if acetate foil is used, as it has two different coloured reflective sides.

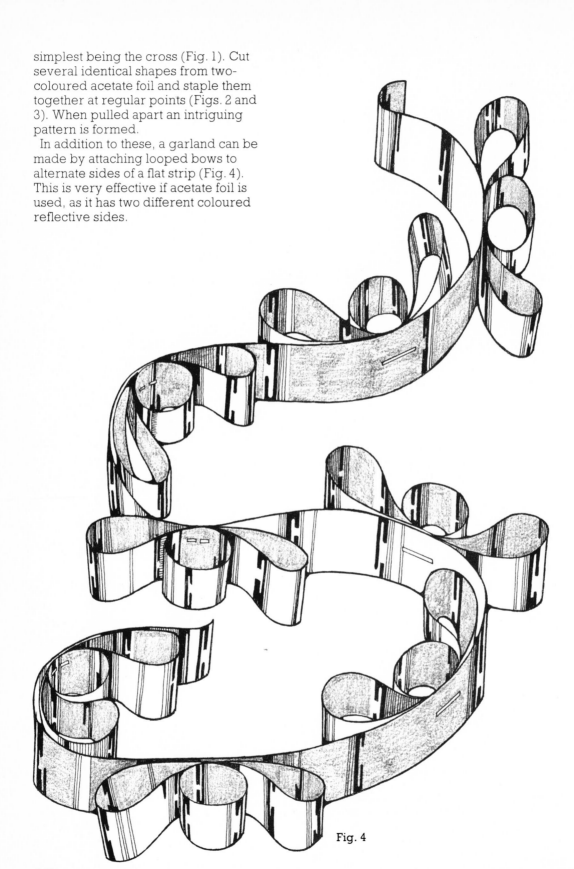

Fig. 4

Christmas Decorations

The Christmas Tree

Of all the events of the year Christmas is the one for which all the greatest efforts are put into decorations, whether they are around the house or on the tree. The charming tradition of decorating a pine tree can be traced back before it was common in Britain. It was a German tradition introduced to this country by Queen Victoria's husband, Prince Albert. The use of pines and other types of evergreens were part of pagan traditions before Christianity and, thankfully, have remained an essential part of decoration providing a refreshing contrast to all the artificial decorations which abound today.

Successfully decorating a tree is an art in itself. The decoration should be a balanced combination of baubles and other hanging ornaments, interlaced with tinsel garlands and festooned with sparkling lights. A reflective material is best for the pendants as it can only be enhanced by the lights. These ornaments can be as intricate as the material allows but the final weight is restricted by the strength of the branch from which they are hung. Whatever the shape of the decoration it should be strung from a piece of thread which allows it to hang absolutely perpendicular, and be free of obstruction so that it can rotate in the warm air-streams created by the lights.

The types of decoration can be divided into three groups, which are: miniature parcels for traditional, little gifts or edible goodies; small figures or personalities such as angels, snowmen, Father Christmas and other characters which are part of the Christmas scene; and the range of abstract decorations such as baubles, pendants, stars, icicles etc.

Miniature Parcels

Many of the parcel wrapping techniques previously described can be adapted in miniature for the tree. For example, a tiny carrier bag can be made to be approximately 2·5 cm (1 in) square in paper-backed foil with handles made from gold thread. This will be the right size for a single chocolate. All the different colours available in paper-backed foil means that carrier bags can always be made to fit in with the general colour scheme of the decorations.

Little boxes can be very intriguing as they conceal their contents. Using foil card the traditional box cube shape can be adapted into all forms of caskets with assorted shapes. The process for making all the caskets is the same.

First cut a strip of foil card 2·5 cm (1 in) wide and curve it into the required shape, creating corners by pinching the card if necessary. Join the ends and secure with glue. Thread a piece of cord through the strip, form a loop and knot it on the inside.

Place the shaped strip onto the piece of card and draw round the inside of the strip, taking care not to dislodge the shape in the process (Fig. 1). Repeat the process for the second size and cut them both out leaving 1 cm (½ in) extra card all round for the lip. Remember that if the chosen shape is not symmetrical the strip will need to be turned over so that the area in the centre is mirrored.

Make regular cuts from the edge of

1–5 The uses of acetate foil are endless and the expanded shapes are particularly attractive.

6, 7 Crepe paper garlands are cheap and quick to make.

A mass of chains and garlands create the right atmosphere for carnivals, Christmas or family celebrations.

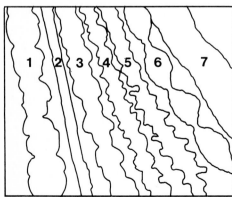

the card up to the pattern line approximately 0·5 cm (¼ in) apart. If there are any acute curves it may be necessary to make a few extra cuts (Fig. 2). Score all round the pattern line and bend all the tabs backwards. Apply glue to these and carefully insert the piece into the strip trying not to distort the original shape. Putting the first piece in is not too difficult, but ensure that the surface is perfectly aligned with the edge of the strip. The second piece is a little more tricky as there is nothing to stop it from falling

into the centre apart from careful handling.

When the casket is completely dry it is ready to hang on the tree as it is, or to acquire some additional decoration in the form of cords or little picture scraps. These caskets particularly lend themselves to the oval shape; an influence from the Victorians.

Some other successful shapes are the circle, square, diamond and kite. Those with curved edges really show the metallic surface of the sides to advantage, and for this reason some of the traditional shapes like a heart, paisley leaf or dewdrop, are the ones to choose. It is interesting to experiment with other shapes and create a host of varying shapes for the tree.

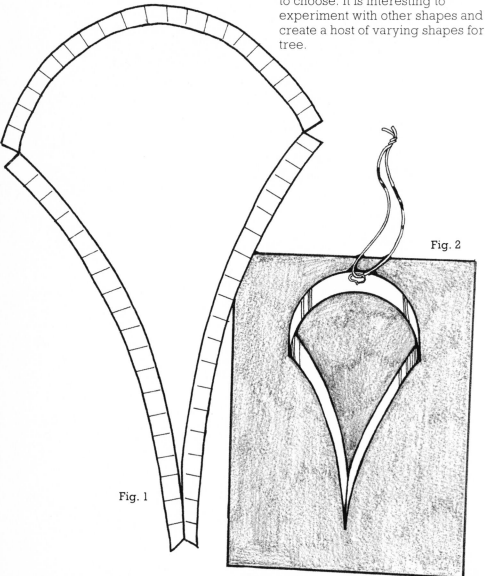

Fig. 2

Fig. 1

152

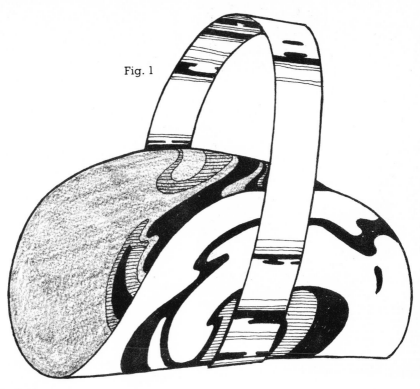

Fig. 1

Miniature Baskets

Little baskets are always a charming way to present sweets and the handle forms a natural point for suspension. There are a great many shapes to choose from: square and round shapes, which look like little buckets, and inverted cones and pyramids. As baskets are made with solid card, the addition of paper doyleys, particularly the foil ones, can be used to create a decorative edging by lining the basket.

One of the simplest shapes to make is the flower basket, which is a disc of card 8 cm (3 in) diameter, and a strip of card 1 cm ($\frac{1}{2}$ in) which is looped round the disc as the handle. Pulling the strip up tightly will curve the disc to form the elegant little display basket shape (Fig. 1). While the basket is suspended from a swaying branch, a little glue may be needed to keep the gift in place.

Although foil card is, of course, the strongest material to use, it may not always be available. Also it may be preferable, particularly for shapes where both sides of the material are visible, to use paper-backed foil double. Two sheets can be glued together, thus allowing the possibility of combining two different colours. For a more professional finish, a can of aerosol glue is the best to use as it will spray a very fine and even layer of glue over the surface.

The two layers of paper assembled in this way are also useful for some of the other three-dimensional decorations. For example, the umbrella-shaped doyley bag which first appeared on page 51 as a gift wrapping for handkerchiefs, can be adapted for the tree by making a miniature version. This will display both sides of the paper to advantage with its curved folds.

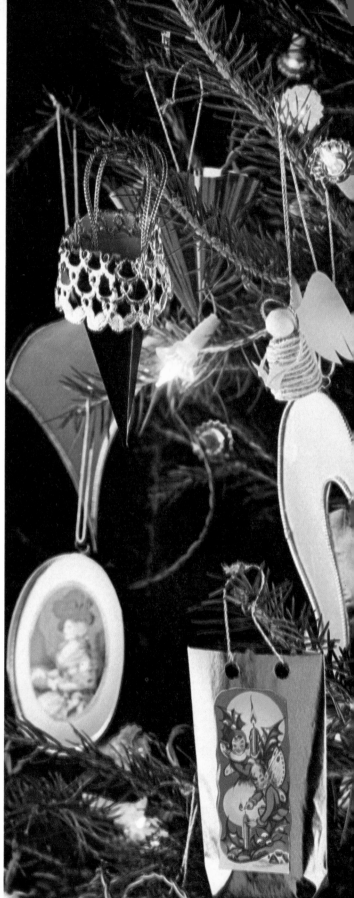

Imaginative use of reflective papers gives
a traditional Christmas tree extra sparkle.
In the centre of the picture is a small foil
bag surrounded by bells, angels, caskets,
miniature carrier bags, baskets and stars.

Christmas Tree Angels

Angels play a very important part, not only in the story of Christmas, but, because of their charming decorative shape, as ornaments also. These little figures are only 5 cm (2 in) tall. A thimble is used to form the mould for the dress itself, with a puffball for the head and, apart from the addition of some gold cord, the only other materials used are cartridge paper, white crepe paper and some glue. Suspended from their thin loops of gold cord they appear to be flying between the branches of the Christmas tree.

To make an angel you will need:—
    A thimble
    1 strip of white crepe paper cut across the roll 1 cm ($\frac{1}{2}$ in) wide
    Cartridge paper 15 cm (6 in) square
    25 cm (10 in) thin gold cord
    4 cm (1$\frac{1}{2}$ in) thicker gold cord
    Puffball 1 cm ($\frac{1}{2}$ in) diameter
    Glue

First cover the thimble with some of the cartridge paper, cutting the shape from the side of the square (Fig. 1) to allow enough paper to make the wings afterwards, and secure with glue. Do not allow any glue to reach the thimble as this is to be removed when the glue has dried.

Meanwhile twist the strip of crepe paper into twine and then, holding both the thin gold cord and the twine together, work the two in a spiral to cover the thimble. Start from the base of the thimble, and work right up the sides over the top until it is entirely covered, securing each end with a little glue (Fig. 2).

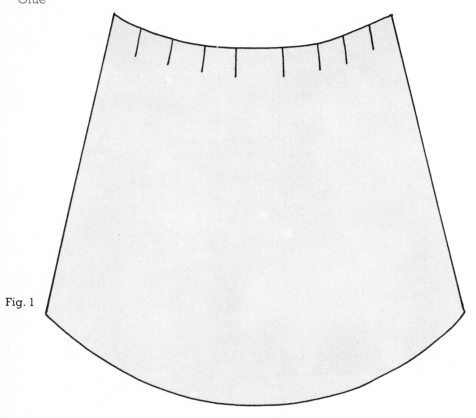

Fig. 1

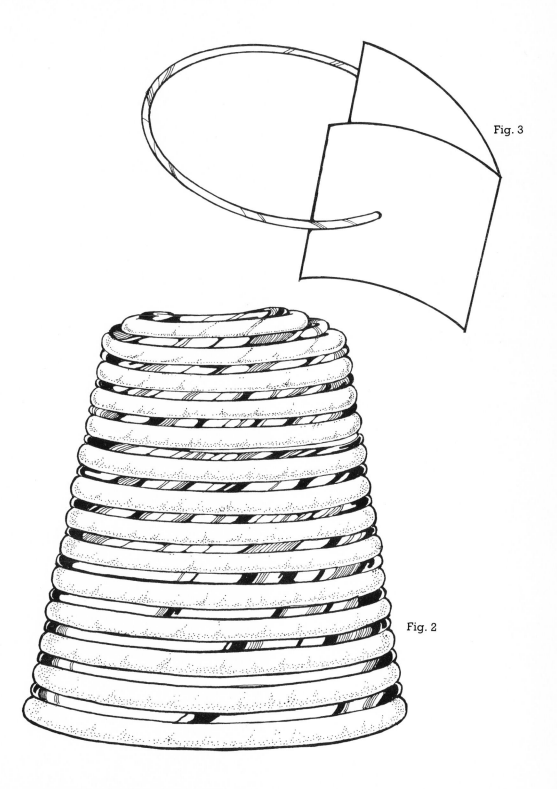

Fig. 3

Fig. 2

Charlie with his cheerful smile and clown-like appearance is sure to appeal to young and old alike. Here the use of different colours and sizes show how he can be adapted to fit the requirements of any home. The miniature Charlie would make a lovely stocking present for a child or even a tree decoration.

Cut the little book shape (Fig. 3) and using another piece of twine cut the length of 4 cm (1½ in) and glue each end to the book and form a loop; these are to represent the arms.

Apply some glue to the base of the puffball and loop the thicker cord so that it forms the halo and press into place (Fig. 4). Using a liberal amount of glue, place the head on top of the thimble; then attach the arms which should be fixed at the back of the neck close to the point where the halo touches the thimble (Fig. 5).

Finally, cut the wing shapes, folding the remaining piece of cartridge paper in half so that the wings are identically shaped (Fig. 6). The folded square from which the wings are cut is 5 cm (2 in). These are attached at the same point as the arms with glue. A thin piece of cord is carefully intertwined between the arms and the head and tied into a loop for suspension.

Fig. 4

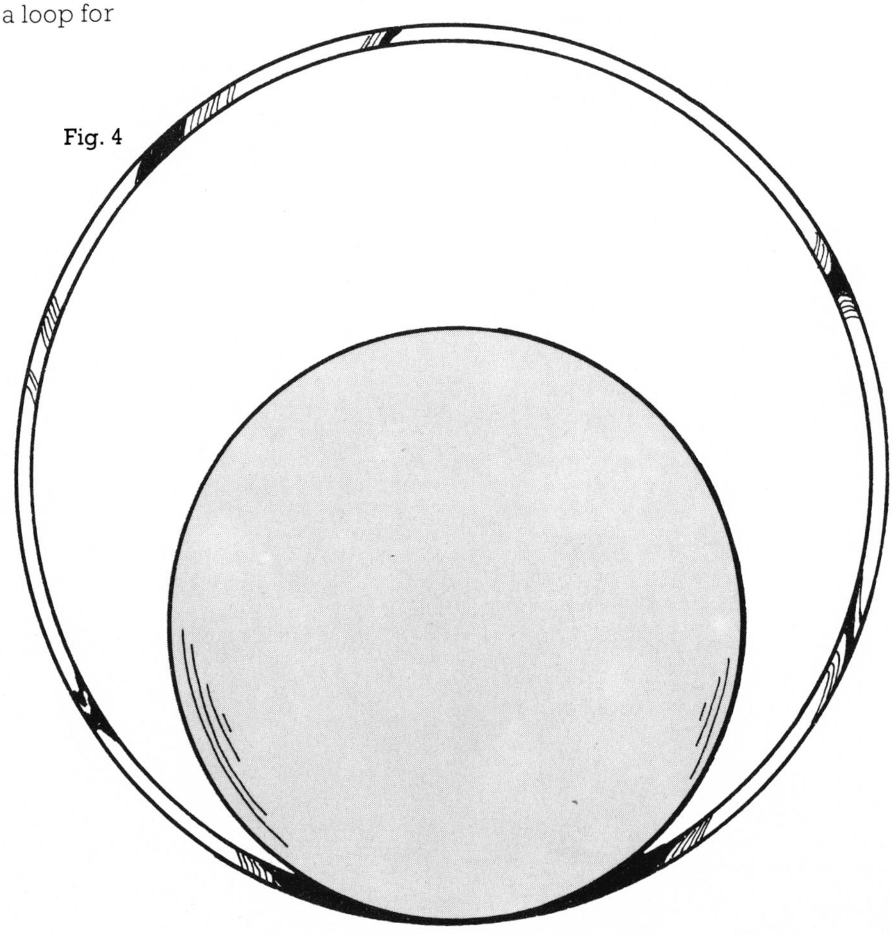

Fig. 6

Fig. 5

Bells

Bells are always associated with religious festivals of all kinds; their cheerful tones can be heard to ring from church towers to relay good news to everyone, so they are particularly relevant at Christmas time. Their natural hanging shape is an invitation in itself to use them as Christmas tree decorations.

One of the simplest ways to produce a realistic shape is to find an actual bell and use it as a mould. Various techniques can be adopted such as papier-mâché, which is probably the most realistic and is very decorative when covered with silver paper. More stylised versions can be made with various papers over similar-shaped moulds. The thimble is a common object which is very similar to a bell and can be used to create delightful little bells which can be suspended from the top of the Christmas tree.

To make a thimble bell you will need:—
    A thimble
    Cartridge paper
    1 piece of crepe paper 1 cm ($\frac{1}{2}$ in) wide cut across the roll
    Silver cord 40 cm (16 in) long
    Silver pendant bead
    Binding wire, 28 gauge, 8 cm (3 in) long
    Glue

First cover the thimble with the cartridge paper and secure with glue. Prepare the paper twine and then using both the silver cord and the twine together work the two in a spiral, starting at the base of the thimble, until the whole surface is covered (Fig. 1).

Thread the bead onto the binding wire and secure by twisting the ends of the wire together, and then make a loop in the top of the wire so that it can be attached to the bell (Fig. 2).

Remove the bell shape from the thimble and make a hole in the top. This should be sufficiently large to thread both ends of the silver cord through it. Once threaded through insert the wire with the bead, passing the cord through the loop at the top of the wire before tying a knot in the cord to secure it all.

The bead should hang perpendicular and free in the centre of the bell and be just visible below its edge (Fig. 3). Adjustments may be necessary to ensure that this is so. These look very attractive hung in pairs of slightly different lengths. They can, of course, be made in various colours and with assorted cords.

162

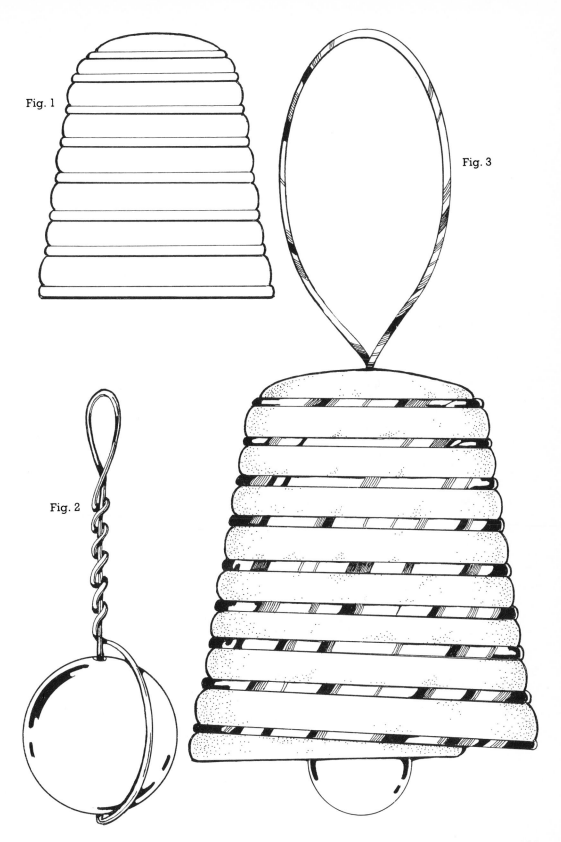

Fig. 1

Fig. 2

Fig. 3

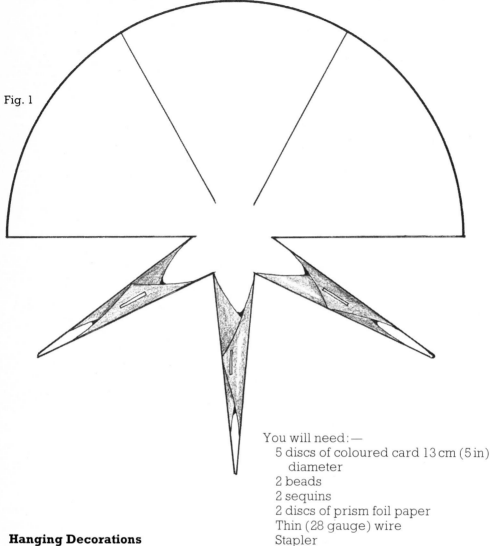

Fig. 1

Hanging Decorations

Stars

Another traditional Christmas
ornament is the star, and here are two
amongst the many which could be
described. Again the choice of
material will control the possible size
of the object. Both these two are made
by threading discs of paper together
centrally in succession above one
another. If a complete sphere is
required it is possible to achieve it by
adding subsequent additional shapes
until the whole area is filled.
How to make the pointed star.

You will need:—
    5 discs of coloured card 13 cm (5 in)
      diameter
    2 beads
    2 sequins
    2 discs of prism foil paper
    Thin (28 gauge) wire
    Stapler
Cut the discs from a circle made with a
compass and then, using the same
radius, mark six equidistant points
around the edge. Join the points to
produce radiating lines and cut in to
within 1 cm ($\frac{1}{2}$ in) of the centre along
each one. Curl the resulting corners of
each fan shape so that the colour is on
the outside. Then to produce a cone
join each pair of corners with a staple
(Fig. 1).
  This makes a single star-shaped layer
with six points. Make the other four in
the same way. Join them all together
by threading a bead, sequin and disc
of prism paper onto the wire and then

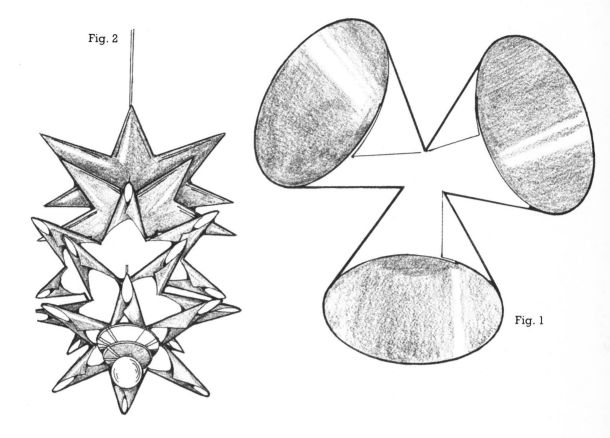

Fig. 2

Fig. 1

through the centre of three of the stars (Fig. 2). Then turn the other two stars so that they face the opposite way and attach them in the same manner. Finally add the second prism disc, sequin and bead, in that order, before bending the end of the wire back to join the other end in the centre. Twist these together and, as the twist tightens, the centre will be drawn in to make the points spring outwards. The wire is used to form the hook.

To make the cone star you will need:—
    6 discs of coloured card 10·5 cm (5 in) wide
    2 beads
    2 sequins
    2 discs of prism foil paper
    Thin (28 gauge) wire
Mark these discs in a similar way to the pointed star but make cuts on every alternate line, so that there are

only three fan shapes. Shape the corners by curling them over with the colour on the outside. Join these so that the point of the cone is in the centre of the disc and the cone is funnel-shaped (Fig. 1).

Make three of these on each disc and assemble all the layers with the beads, sequins and prism papers, using the identical method to the pointed star. Because of the number of layers this star is more spherical in shape than the pointed one.

For a variation this could be made with cartridge paper with decorated edges to emphasise the cones. Both stars make a delicate decoration when made in miniature with tissue paper.

Quilled Mobile

Quilling is a form of three-dimensional papercraft which lends itself to moving suspension. The process, explained earlier, can be applied to free-hanging designs which are suitable for Christmas decorations or for the tree. Whether placed onto a lacy paper backing, or simply used by themselves, the inter-play of patterns can be intriguing. From delicate paper ones which can be beautiful, to strong coverpaper ones which require staples for security, the range of sizes can be quite dramatic. The most suitable paper to use for Christmas decorations of this sort is two-coloured acetate foil. The size will be controlled by the strength of the paper.

Charlie

This little person is a great favourite with children and is a happy addition to the Christmas scene. He can be adapted to any size and the size of head varies accordingly. He was originally designed after a request to make something with Christmas material so pieces of tinsel, a Christmas bauble or similar substitute, and frills from the crackers are the main materials used.

To make Charlie you will need:—
    4 18 in stem wires
    1 12 in stem wire
    2 tinsel garlands
    1 bauble or puffball
    Foil card for his hands, feet and hat
    Sequins for his facial features
    Strip of crepe paper 12·5 cm (5 in) wide cut from the bottom of the roll
    Binding wire
    Binding tape
    Glue
First cover the long stem wires with tape and make an open hook on the top of each one (Fig. 1).
  Cut out four hand shapes and four feet shapes from the foil card, approximately 9 cm (3½ in) long. Remember to cut two of each facing the opposite way otherwise he may

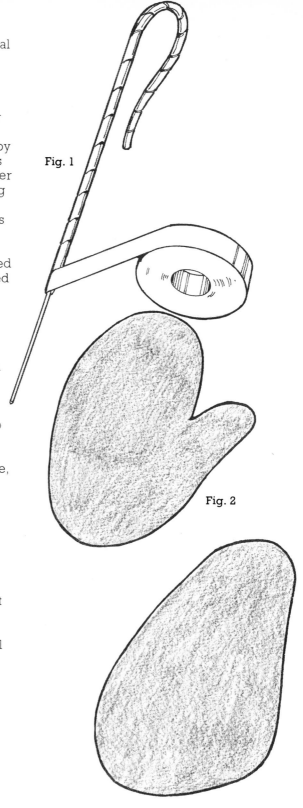

Fig. 1

Fig. 2

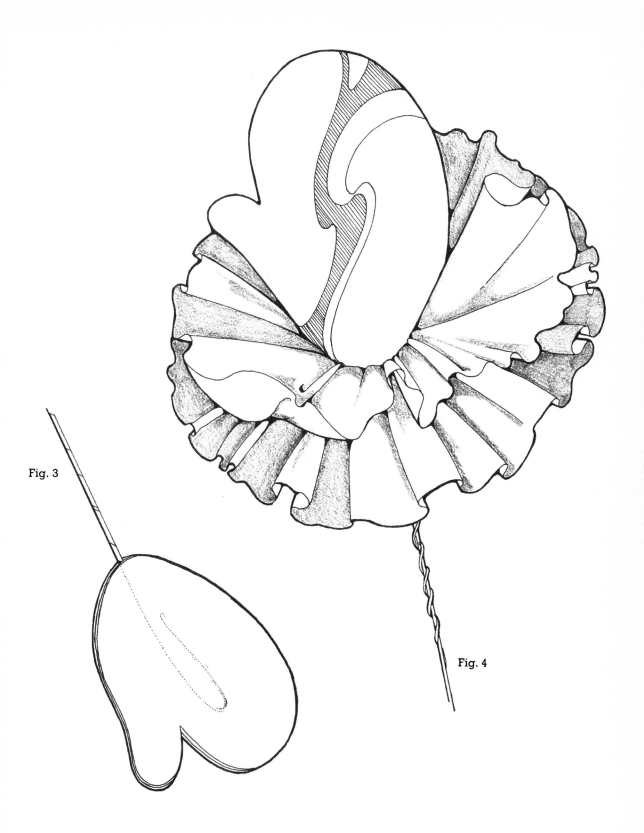

Fig. 3

Fig. 4

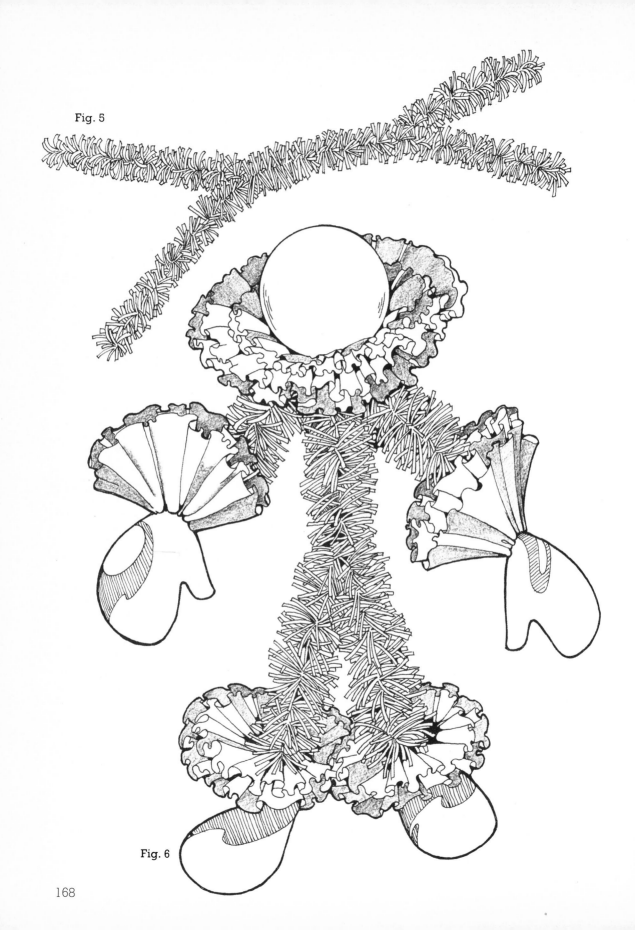

Fig. 5

Fig. 6

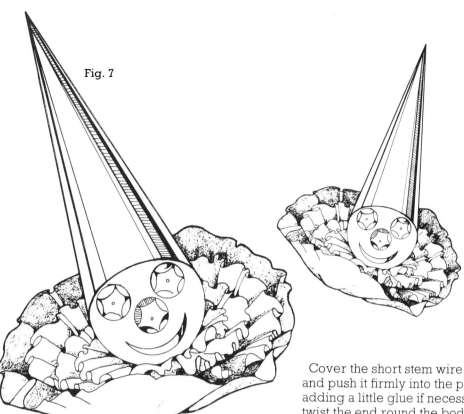

Fig. 7

land up with two left feet (Fig. 2). Apply glue to the entire surface of one hand and glue another to it back to back, sandwiching the wire between the two (Fig. 3).

Frill all along both sides of the strip of crepe paper and cut off some lengths of 30 cm (12 in). Fold each one in half lengthways and, placing the binding wire inside the fold, gather the frill together and fix it to a wrist or ankle by binding the spare wire round the limb itself (Fig. 4). Repeat the process with the other hands and feet.

Cover the limbs by binding them with tinsel garland and twist the top half of the pair of legs together. Twist the arms together in the same way and then twist the arms and legs together to form a spread-eagled body shape (Fig. 5).

Cover the short stem wire with tinsel and push it firmly into the puffball adding a little glue if necessary. Then twist the end round the body to fix the head into place.

Cut two more pieces from the strip of paper 40 cm (16 in) long, and place one on top of the other, slightly overlapping, and fold them over lengthways together. Insert the binding wire into the fold and gather it together until it fits round his neck. Attach it by twisting the ends of the wire together (Fig. 6).

Cut a fan-shaped piece of foil card for his hat, radius 20 cm (8 in) and coil it into a cone shape, overlapping the join until it fits his head. Secure with glue.

Finally bring him to life by adding sequins for his eyes, nose and mouth, fixing them on with a little glue (Fig. 7). The mouth is a large flat gypsy sequin which is cut to a smiling shape, although in the absence of these sequins it is quite possible to cut the shapes from paper-backed foil.

Charlie can be a cheerful Christmas playmate or a smiling welcome to the house. In miniature he makes a charming decoration for the tree.

List of Stockists

All the companies listed below will supply a catalogue and goods by mail order.

Great Britain

E. J. Arnold & Son Ltd. Butterly Street Leeds	Paper, glue, paints, boards
Craftsmiths The Guildhall Development Exeter Devon	Flower-making materials, cutters, pots, glue, paper
Ells & Farrier 2 Princes Street Hanover Square London W.1	Beads, puffballs, sequins
Hobby Horse Ltd. 15-17 Langton Street London S.W.10	Beads and sequins
Paperchase Ltd. 216 Tottenham Court Road London W.1	Paper of all kinds
Stonleigh Mail Order Company 91 Prince Avenue Southend-on-Sea Essex	Cracker materials
The Whookey Hole Mill Whookey Hole Near Wells, Somerset	Hand-made papers. Tours of the mill also available all the year round.

Pamela Woods Mail Order
80 Shakespeare Avenue
Bath
Avon

Flower-making materials,
Charlie kit, cracker kits,
beads

The following companies, in addition to supplying goods by mail order will
advise on the address of your nearest stockist.

Australia
Handcraft Supply Pty. Ltd.
P.O. Box 3
33 Brighton Avenue,
Croydon Park,
New South Wales 2133

Canada
Lewiscraft
40 Commander Boulevard
Agincourt
Ontario

New Zealand
Golding Industries Handicraft Centre
158 Cuba Street
Wellington

Index